PAGE STREET
PUBLISHING CO.

Copyright © 2018 Clint Edwards

First published in 2018 by
Page Street Publishing Co.
27 Congress Street, Suite 105
Salem, MA 01970
www.pagestreetpublishing.com

Distributed by Macmillan, sales in Canada by The Canadian Manda Group.

22   21   20   19   18   1   2   3   4   5

ISBN-13: 978-1-62414-532-2
ISBN-10: 1-62414-532-9

Library of Congress Control Number: 2017955968

Cover Image: Istock/CSA-Printstock
Cover and Interior Design: Page Street Publishing Inc.

Printed and bound in the United States

Eleven Years in, and I Finally See How Amazing My Wife Looks in a Nice Restaurant; I Wasn't Man Enough to Witness Childbirth; It Goes by Pretty Fast. Stop and Look Around © Disney. Reprinted by permission of *Disney Online*. All Rights Reserved.

I'M SORRY...
LOVE, YOUR HUSBAND

HONEST, HILARIOUS STORIES
FROM A FATHER OF THREE WHO MADE
<u>ALL</u> THE MISTAKES (AND MADE UP FOR THEM)

CLINT EDWARDS
WRITER FOR SCARY MOMMY

PAGE STREET
PUBLISHING CO.

FOR TRISTAN, NORAH AND ASPEN:
Someday I want you to read this, so you
will know that although I often told you
I knew everything, you will realize that
I honestly and truly didn't.

"Mawage.

Mawage is wot bwings us togeder today.

Mawage, that bwessed awangment,

that dweam wifin a dweam."

—THE PRINCESS BRIDE

TABLE OF WRONGNESS

PREGNANCY AND CHILDBIRTH 127

PARENTING 179

"DON'T YOU THINK YOU'RE OVERREACTING?"

Okay, I lied to you. This isn't a chapter. It's actually the preface to the book. Perhaps I shouldn't start a book with a lie, so I'm sorry. I apologize. Please forgive me. I'll never do it again. But here's the thing. *Preface* is such a boring title, and I don't think anyone reads the preface of any book. But that doesn't mean this preface, my preface, isn't important, because it is. So I lied. Just a small one. An insignificant, no-big-deal, you-can-still-love-me lie. If I told you that I had a three-headed dog, you'd realize that I didn't as soon as you got into the circus tent. But, hey. Stay and look around, because you are about to meet the biggest circus in the history of ever . . . my family.

OK, wait. Perhaps I am exaggerating. Which isn't a lie . . . exactly. It's a bending of the truth. My family is actually pretty normal. I think. I hope. Mel and I have been married since 2004. We have three kids, Tristan (the know it all), Norah (the snarky princess), and Aspen (the worst roommate ever). All of them are amazing and frustrating and completely overwhelming.

I don't really know what I'm doing as a father and husband, so I apologize a lot. But, honestly, does anyone know what they are doing? I doubt it. And don't look online for answers. No family's house is as clean as their Facebook pictures show. They just move the laundry pile to another chair, out of view, along with the Play-Doh and Pokémon cards. And no one's children are all that respectful, regardless of how perfect their parenting is. Sometimes the children are sweet. But sometimes they're jerks, too. Just like everyone else. And there is, in fact, no official parenting manual, because raising a family is actually a million gears turning in a million different directions, all of them covered in sour milk.

So, yeah, sometimes it feels like I'm running a circus. In fact, as I'm writing this preface, Aspen is sucking milk from her sippy cup and spitting it at the TV. It's her new thing. We are working through it.

Okay, I lied again. I'm sorry. She's actually at daycare. Probably spitting milk at their TV.

Are you mad I lied again? Oh, come on. Don't you think you're overreacting? Sorry. Scratch that.

Family, marriage, all of it, has caused me to make some mistakes. A lot of them, actually. I've said a lot of things I shouldn't have said, like, "Don't you think you're overreacting?".

(Sorry again about that.)

I've felt guilty over everything from getting flaming pissed because my son farted on me, to letting him blow all of his birthday money, to my messy house, to missing all the naps. But ultimately, much of parenting and marriage is about mistakes and apologies and feeling inadequate. (I'm sorry, but it's true.) It's about recognizing when you're wrong, saying you're sorry, learning from your mistakes, and hoping and praying that you didn't just screw up your child for life or lose your spouse. And when I think about all this, I realize that perhaps it was best for me to start this book with a mistake—and an apology.

It makes sense, doesn't it?

Although, I will say it: Moms are rock stars. Mel is the most amazing woman I know. She is smart and driven and, most importantly, she calls me on my crap in ways that infuriate me in the moment but help me realize that she loves me enough to try to make me a better husband and father. What could be more loving than that?

Perhaps I should have titled this book *Listen to Your Wife*.

No . . . I like my first title.

Going into marriage, I didn't see our arguments as a show of love. It took me years to see it that way. Even now, I struggle to see my own shortcomings. But that's being human, right? So I'm going to talk Mel up, because she's the most wonderful thing in my life.

Hands down.

I hope you don't mind.

Mel has made mistakes, too, though. No doubt about it. But those are her stories, and these are mine. Someday she might write a book titled *I'm Sorry . . . Love, Your Wife*. But right now, these are my apologies; these are my mistakes.

So buckle up.

If you are a wife and mother reading this, I know you will see a lot of similarities between your husband, my dumbassery and Mel's frustrations. And if you are a father and husband reading this, hopefully you can learn from my mistakes and better understand that although marriage and family is life changing in the most frustrating ways, it is all completely worth it. And if you are a child reading this, I hope you asked your parents' permission, because it might freak you out and cause you to never get married and/or have children. This book is a real and honest look at the fact that raising you little turds is the most difficult thing in the history of ever. But that doesn't make it bad; it makes parenting worth it.

And if you are a fan of *No Idea What I'm Doing: A Daddy Blog* (my site), or if you are one of the bazillion people who follow me on social media and have been grooving to the articles I've written for *Scary Mommy*, the *Washington Post*, *Babble* and the many other places I've contributed to over the years, you might see a few things you recognize. Some of these chapters were inspired by work I did elsewhere, and I decided to expand them here. It was one of the most exciting parts about writing this book. Online, I am usually left cramming my ideas into 1,000 words or less. But with a book, that rule goes out the window. It's been awesome to expand, mix and weave some of those essays that hit home online, but I felt needed much, much more. There's a lot of new stuff too, so don't worry. You are going to love it!

If you are new to my writing and to the Edwards family, don't you worry at all. You are about to feel a lot better about your marriage and your parenting, because, trust me, I don't know what the hell I'm doing either.

MARRiAGE

THE NOSY NEIGHBOR
AND OUR MESSY HOUSE

I was building shelves in the garage when our neighbor girl, one of my four-year-old daughter's nosy friends, approached me and said, "I just saw in your house. It's pretty dirty. Norah's mommy needs to clean more."

She was a curly-haired, blond-headed little five-year-old in jeans and a brightly colored T-shirt who often ventured from her yard into ours. When I say often, I mean several times a day. We lived in a small neighborhood in rural Oregon, population 1,600. Kids didn't wander neighborhoods like they did when I was a kid back in the '80s, when we went from house to house, sometimes miles from home, looking for someone to play with. But they definitely ventured a house or two over. The house next to us was a rental, and that's where this girl was living. She was one of two families who'd ended up living next to us over the past couple of years, and this wasn't the first time she'd peeked in our windows. She had a nasty habit of doing that, regardless of the day and time.

CRAP LIKE THIS SEEMED CHARMING IN SHOWS LIKE LEAVE IT TO BEAVER, BUT IN REAL LIFE IT'S INCREDIBLY IRRITATING TO HAVE SOME LITTLE KID PEEKING IN ON YOUR EVERY MOMENT...

It was a common occurrence for me to look up from my meal, my family seated at the dinner table, and see this young lady gazing at me from the window next to the dining room. It's funny, really. Crap like this seemed charming in shows like *Leave It to Beaver*, but in real life it's incredibly irritating to have some little kid peeking in on your every moment, asking if your daughter can play and making snide comments about your home.

I did have empathy for her, however. Her mother was single, and she worked a full-time job. In a lot of ways, her situation reminded me of the one I grew up in. And I think that's the main reason I never approached this girl's parent. As irritating as she was, I didn't want to add more stress to a single mother.

Ironically, just the day before this little girl commented on the state of our house, Mel and I had discussed putting curtains in our front windows to keep her from peeking inside. We hadn't gotten around to it, however, so now this nosy little neighbor was placing my wife on trial for keeping a messy house. She had a hand on her hip, eyes open wide, waiting for a response.

THE SUCKIEST PART ABOUT WHAT FIVE-YEAR-OLDS SAY IS THAT THEY ARE 100 PERCENT HONEST.

"Some people find comments like that rude," I said.

She looked at me with a snarky smile and said, "Yup!"

The suckiest part about what five-year-olds say is that they are 100 percent honest. And, indeed, our house was a mess. At the time, I could've probably listed a million reasons why we had clutter piles, random installments of underwear, laundry baskets full of clean laundry sitting precariously in the middle of the living room, cracker crumbs spackled about the carpet, and so on. There always seemed to be a bracelet loom, a couple of dolls, a Play-Doh kit and a few dirty dishes on the table. The sink was often full of dishes, and our garage was a wreck of boxes. The reason I was building shelves was to try to add some order to the chaos.

Because of the rental houses next door and the one across the street, the number of children in our neighborhood waxed and waned. At this particular time, we were at an all-time neighbor kids high. The rental across the street had a family with five or six kids. I honestly don't know how many children really lived there. Perhaps they were cousins or stepkids. They all had the same brown hair and eyes. I'm not the kind of person to get to know my neighbors, so I simply assumed they all came from the brown-haired, brown-eyed adults who lived in the home. For all I know, though, they could have been running an orphanage. I couldn't keep track of all the children entering and exiting that house. The nosy little girl's family next door had another five kids. For the past several months we always had random kids hanging out in our living room, on the porch or in my children's rooms, eating our food and making messes by getting out our toys and not putting them back.

My two older children, Tristan and Norah, loved it.

Mel and I didn't.

We'd also just had a new baby, Aspen, which was easily the biggest (and best) reason for our messy house. Few things are as disruptive as a new baby, and considering Mel and I were struggling to handle the transition from two kids to three, which truthfully felt like I was juggling chain saws and someone asked me to hold a baby, our house was exceptionally bad. Not that we had piles of garbage or anything particularly nasty like that. It was kid clutter and some dirty dishes. It's the stuff that people crop out of the background when posting pictures of their family on Facebook or shove into another room when inviting company. But this nosy little girl, peeking in our windows, got the full reality of our mess, and she was more than happy to tell my wife, who was currently recovering from a cesarean, that she needed to get her act together.

MEL AND I WERE STRUGGLING TO HANDLE THE TRANSITION FROM TWO KIDS TO THREE, WHICH TRUTHFULLY FELT LIKE I WAS JUGGLING CHAIN SAWS AND SOMEONE ASKED ME TO HOLD A BABY

At least in her case, I can give her the benefit of the doubt. She was five years old. She didn't really understand the realities of parenting and family. I hadn't taken the time to peek in her windows, so I didn't know the state of her house, but I had to assume that it wasn't much better than ours. I mean, honestly, if she and her siblings were half as inconsiderate and messy at their own home as they were in our home, their house had to look like a garbage truck crashed into a rummage sale.

Her older brother didn't even knock anymore. This ten-year-old dark-haired sports enthusiast who predominantly wore brightly colored off-brand sports clothing with captions like *Football Is Life* and *Pass Me the Ball* once walked into my house, poured himself a glass of milk, drank half of it, left the jug along with the half-empty glass on the counter and then walked out. I was sitting on the sofa folding laundry as he did it. I assumed he was there to play with my eight-year-old son, Tristan, but he wasn't. He just wanted some milk.

What a dick move.

I MEAN, HONESTLY, IF SHE AND HER SIBLINGS WERE HALF AS INCONSIDERATE AND MESSY AT THEIR OWN HOME AS THEY WERE IN OUR HOME, THEIR HOUSE HAD TO LOOK LIKE A GARBAGE TRUCK CRASHED INTO A RUMMAGE SALE.

I mean, seriously, were we an open kitchen? The least he could have done was put the milk away. Wait, the least he could have done was knock and ask for something to drink. Wait, wait, the least he could have done was put up the toilet seat when he peed at my house.

I suppose that's a different story altogether.

The whole milk situation made me feel walked on, and to top it all off, his sister felt that we had a messy house. I know that some kids are better or worse behaved when at other people's homes, but what Mel and I later referred to as Milkgate 2014 went down in the history books of jackass neighbor-kid moves.

Sometimes I daydreamed of walking into the home next door and pulling the same milk-drinking action. Or perhaps just looking in their windows and making snide comments.

Or maybe peeing on their toilet seat.

But the problem is, I'm an adult now, so I have to take these sorts of things with a grain of salt. I have to be understanding and grown-up about it all, even in moments when I really, really don't want to.

And yet, with all the factors coming at us—new baby, young children, crappy neighbor kids—I still felt ashamed of our messy house. I think that's the really frustrating part about clean-house judgment. I think most families aren't all that much better at keeping their house tidy than Mel and I are. They are simply better at hiding it. They are more diligent about tucking things in back rooms and cleaning the visible spots. And perhaps that's what I'd find by looking in my neighbors' windows, a clean living room, while the rest of the house looked as bad, or even worse, than my own.

I don't know if it's part of a parent's genetics to try to give excuses for a messy house, or if it's something we all learn growing up. All parents since the history of ever have felt the shame of judgment when a visitor, regardless of his or her age, has given their messy house that snide, twisted-lip look that seems to say, "I just saw in your house. It's pretty dirty."

And while my house was messy on the day of the little girl's comment, there are people with messier houses. I've seen them. And when I was young, I'd go to these houses and say rotten things like, "I just saw in your house. It's pretty dirty," same as that little girl.

And I think that is part of what drove me so crazy about her. I saw so much of my childhood in her judgmental snarky little butt face. I felt confident that she ran home each evening after peeking in my windows and told her mother all about our mess, half of which she and her siblings assisted with. Then she and her mother would laugh and laugh and judge their messy-house neighbors. Then her mother might say something like, "If she really loved her family, she'd clean the house more."

My mother used to say crap like that.

Obviously it scarred me for life. But I think it scarred mothers most of all. Because the thing is, it always comes down to blaming the mother.

I think that is one of the things that bothered me the most about what that little girl said in my garage. She blamed Mel for our messy house, like I used to.

I'm not happy about it.

I'll tell you that right now.

Shortly after Mel became a stay-at-home mom, I started getting really judgmental. This was about five years earlier, when Mel and I moved to Minnesota for me to attend graduate school. We had two kids then, and with my graduate stipend, scholarships, student loans and the lower cost of living in the Midwest, combined with all the time demands of graduate school, it made sense for Mel to quit her job at the Home Depot, and stay home with the kids. We were both 26 at the time and had been married for about four years. Mel staying home with the kids was something she'd longed for during the majority of our marriage. And while I was happy to have her home with the kids, I started looking at the state of the house and thinking, "You have one job! One job! To take care of the home."

We lived in a three-bedroom townhouse. It was just over 1,000 square feet, and it was the largest house we'd ever lived in. When I came home from school or work, I often made snide comments about the dishes or the toys or the crackers on the carpet. I sounded a lot like the nosy girl next door.

I never really confronted her head-on; it was always something said under my breath, a childish bite at her performance as a mother. At the time, it was my way of dropping a not-so-subtle hint without taking the issue head-on.

When I think back on these comments, however, I realize I was completely spineless. And insensitive.

I often took the snide comment route early in our marriage. I think a lot of men do, hopeful that by making snide remarks we can incite change. However, it doesn't really work that way. What actually happened is it made Mel feel insecure, and it made me look like a judgmental prick (take notes, new fathers).

ALTHOUGH I'D BEEN A FATHER FOR ALMOST THREE YEARS AND FELT LIKE I HAD IT DOWN, I WAS, WITHOUT A DOUBT, A ROOKIE.

Part of the problem with this transition of Mel staying home with the kids was a lack of understanding. Although I'd been a father for almost three years and felt like I had it down, I was, without a doubt, a rookie. Case in point: I didn't understand what it meant to take care of children full-time. I'd never experienced it. Our oldest was about to turn three, and while I'd been an active parent, between college and work I was always a part-time father. And Mel, she was a rookie, too. She'd always been a full-time employee and a part-time mother. Our son had been raised in part by Mel, me and my mother-in-law.

But with our move to Minnesota, that all changed. We had no family. It was just us, and now Mel was a full-time mom, and I was a full-time student and breadwinner. And that all added up to me leaning on the assumption that Mel should be some June Cleaver of a housekeeper and mother, as if that were an actual realistic goal.

I DON'T WANT TO SPEAK FOR ALL KIDS, BUT MY KIDS ARE REMARKABLE MESS MAKERS.

I never considered that my kids don't care if we recently dusted or swept or vacuumed. They'll drop Cheerios anyway. When I was a stay-at-home dad a few years later, I'd sweep beneath the table, and ten minutes later it would be dirty again. I'd have the kids put their toys away before going to bed, and by morning, before I even got up, they were back out.

I don't want to speak for all kids, but my kids are remarkable mess makers.

About six months into Mel being a stay-at-home mom, she finally had enough of my snide comments, and we got into an argument about the house. I told her it was embarrassing. I asked her what she did all day. "It really can't be that hard to keep the house clean," I said.

We got into a huge fight. Mel told me that I needed to realize what she was up against. And then she told me something that really hit home. She said, "Sometimes it comes down to cleaning the house or taking Tristan and Norah to the park, spending time having fun with them, or teaching them to read or write. Sometimes I can either do the dishes, or teach our son how to ride a bike or our daughter how to walk. I'd rather do those things, frankly. I'd rather not be that mom who ignores our kids and myself because I'm so busy worrying about what the neighbors might think of our messy house."

It was then that I stopped looking at the dirty dishes and assuming that they were evidence of Mel sitting around all day. Instead, I got up myself and started washing the dishes. I realized that this was not her mess but our mess, and I started pitching in more.

I stopped worrying about the house and started paying attention to the development of our children. I started to pay attention to how happy they were and the kind of relationship they shared with their mother, and I noticed that we had a messy house and really happy, bright kids.

That's what really matters.

The weekend after our nosy neighbor commented on the state of my house, I was hanging curtains in our front windows as she peeked in and asked what I was doing. It was a warm day in Oregon, so the widows were open. Her blond curls were in pigtails making her appear innocent enough, but behind her eyes and dimpled smile I could see it coming, some crappy, dickhead comment that she couldn't keep to herself.

"Looks like your house is still messy," she said. Then she tilted her head down and to the side, her lips twisted, eyes looking up, as though she'd told me some undeniable truth. "If Norah's mom really loved her, she'd clean the house more."

I took a breath.

I wanted to take a drink.

I stopped what I was doing and stepped outside.

I walked past the nosy neighbor girl.

SHE LOOKED UP AT ME WITH A CURIOUS DIMPLED GRIN, AND I'LL ADMIT, PART OF ME WANTED TO SMACK THIS KID.

In front of our house were two cement steps at the end of our patio. I sat down and then patted the seat next to me. She took a seat. She was in pink shorts that rested just above the knee. Her shins were bruised from playing outside, and her shoes were pink and covered in pictures of Disney princesses that matched her off-white *Frozen* T-shirt. She looked up at me with a curious dimpled grin, and I'll admit, part of me wanted to smack this kid.

I mean, I wouldn't. I never would, but I was flaming pissed. But here's where things get complicated with little kids, even the ones that aren't yours. Her face was soft and sweet and innocent. She was a cute kid, no doubt about it, and I can say with 100 percent conviction that God made children cute because of situations like this. It's the only way they could possibly survive into adulthood.

"Let me tell you something," I said. Then I paused for a moment, trying to figure out what I was going to say to this little girl so that she would understand. "The mess isn't Norah's mommy's mess. It's our family's mess. Norah's mommy doesn't own that mess. In fact, sometimes it's your mess because you are over here so often."

She continued to give me a blank, grinning stare.

"And even if it was Norah's mommy's mess, Norah's mom spends a lot of time making sure that Norah is happy. She spends a lot of time making sure that Norah and her brother are learning new things and growing up to be the best Norah and Tristan they can be. She also just had a baby, which isn't easy at all. And you know what?"

"What," she said.

"I think all of that is more important than a clean house. So if our house is messy, it's because we are spending that time with our children. And that's not a bad thing. It's actually a really good thing. Does that make sense?"

She thought about what I had said for a moment, her blue eyes moving side to side in her little skull. Something seemed to be clicking. She looked up at me with bright eyes and a wholesome crooked-toothed smile and said, "Nope!"

Then she walked across our driveway, down the sidewalk and into her own house.

I put my face in my hands for a moment, elbows resting on my knees. Then I stood and turned around. In the window, holding our new daughter, was Mel with the half grin that wives make only when they realize their husband finally understands.

DAD CAN STAY HOME
WITH SICK KIDS, TOO,
YA KNOW?

I worked longer shifts at my university job during the week so I could take Fridays off and be home alone and write. I was working on this book, actually. Only it wasn't working out like I'd planned. Each Friday before Mel headed to her new teaching gig at our kids' charter school, she'd hand me a list of honey-dos. Or a kid would come down with a cold, and I'd be home trying to write while cooking chicken noodle soup and listening to Tristan or Norah moan as if they were dying, "Can you get me waaaater? I'm toooooo sick to get up." Moments later I'd hear them let out a long healthy laugh at something funny on the iPad. They were milking it to stay home from school longer.

I'm not an idiot. I did the same thing as a kid. We all did.

LEAVE IT TO MY DAUGHTER TO COME UP WITH SOME DRAMATIC ONE-LINER THAT WOULD MAKE ME FEEL LIKE A COMPLETE DICKHEAD. THIS REALLY WAS HER SPECIALTY.

Four Fridays into my new Fridays-off writing arrangement, Norah didn't want to go to the school after care and asked me to pick her up in the early afternoon. I had a looming deadline, and when I told Norah, "No. I've got work to do," her eyes got all misty beneath her brown bangs. Her short, slender frame was in a red school polo with a blue skirt and leggings with kittens on them. She was even missing her two front teeth. She was seven, and everything about her played on my fatherly empathy. Then she said, "If you really loved me, you'd come pick me up."

Leave it to my daughter to come up with some dramatic one-liner that made me feel like a complete dickhead. This really was her specialty.

She ran into her room and slammed the door.

I was wrangling Aspen, our toddler, into clothing during my conversation with Norah, which is always a little stressful. Dressing Aspen was a lot like wrestling a squirmy alligator into pants. Biting and all. Mel heard all of this from the bathroom, and she came down the hall in black slacks and a gray cardigan, half her hair straightened, the other half still mashed from sleep, and said, "Really, Clint? You can't take a fifteen-minute break to pick up your daughter?"

My bags were packed. I was on a guilt trip.

Normally Mel doesn't come at me like this, but she was obviously still a little pissed from the night before. We'd argued because Norah's ear started hurting after dinner. The kid was prone to ear infections, and we weren't sure if she was going to need to stay home during the day. The argument wasn't over the ear, though. It was over who was going to miss work if Norah stayed home.

I had assumed Mel'd stay home. But I suppose I always assume that, which really was the backbone of the problem. We were in the bedroom during our argument.

MY BAGS WERE PACKED. I WAS ON A GUILT TRIP.

"Why does it always fall on me?" she said. "Every time a kid is sick, I'm the one home with them. I'm the one missing work. I mean, honestly, have you ever, even once, stayed home from work with a sick kid?"

I was positive; 100 percent sure that I had.

Hadn't I?

I thought and thought as Mel glared and glared.

She waited for an answer while I searched for one. I gave her a couple of half starts,

"What about . . ."

"There was the one day . . ."

"I stayed home from class once . . . didn't I?"

Then I finally conceded.

"I can't remember a *specific time*, but I'm pretty sure I have."

I ASSUMED MY CERTAINTY WOULD MAKE UP FOR MY SPARSE AND ULTIMATELY PATHETIC ANSWER . . .

I said it with a stern confidence, emphasizing *specific* and *time* to give my argument weight. I assumed my certainty would make up for my sparse and ultimately pathetic answer, and cause Mel to drop the argument.

It didn't work.

I'm as surprised as you are.

Thinking back, though, I probably sounded like the last time my son insisted he flushed the toilet, but the evidence told a different story.

She didn't say anything. Instead, she gave me the mom look: a piercing, never-wavering stare that all moms have. My mother had this look. And so did my grandmother. When I got married, I'd assumed I'd escape it, but I was wrong.

I looked at the carpet.

Mel stepped into the bathroom.

Part of the problem was that Mel working was a new thing for us. We'd gone through several arrangements over the years. When we first had Tristan, we both worked while I went to school. But once I went to grad school, Mel became a stay-at-home mom. Then once I was done with school, Mel went back to finish her degree. Suddenly she was a stay-at-home mom and student, while I started my big-kid, after-college job at the university. With each transition, the game changed when it came to childcare, and I will be the first to admit that each change had never gone smoothly. Thinking about all this, it seems like we should have gotten better at these transitions, but we hadn't.

In some ways we've gotten suckier.

So now, with Mel working outside the home, we were in the middle of changing again, and, naturally, I was about to say something stupid.

"Well . . . okay. So maybe I haven't. But it's easier for you to miss work," I said. "And I make more money."

Poof.

The air shot from the room.

Gone.

I was suffocating.

I felt hot around my collar for some reason. It was almost as if the universe knew I'd said something stupid, and suddenly the stars and the earth were out of balance.

Mel stepped back into the room and looked at me, and I realized we'd moved past the mom look into something altogether new and frightening. She looked at me as though she were an iceberg and I was the *Titanic*.

I was going down, down, down . . .

"So that makes my work less important?" she said. "Why does it always fall on me? When I was in school, I still had to take care of the kids when they got sick." She went on about how she had to change their puke bowls while studying for chemistry. And now that she's at work, if one of the kids gets sick, she still takes care of them.

Always.

"You go to work, and I'm left with everything. It's like I added a part-time job to my full-time job. Just because you make more doesn't mean that you're not still a father."

I started to say something, but it came out as a stammer. Then Mel cut me off with this, "It's not about money." She was pointing at me now. The left side of her hair in a wavy lump upon her head, supported by a large brown hair clip. She was in gray leggings with white crew socks, pink worn Crocs and an old T-shirt with the caption *Ketchup Totally Counts as a Vegetable*. She looked comical, no doubt about it, but what she said hit me hard.

"When you started writing, you didn't make any money, and I still watched the kids so you could write. It's about you thinking that what you do is more important than anything I do, and that anything to do with childcare during your work hours is my responsibility."

Then she walked out of our bedroom and slammed the bedroom door.

We went to sleep angry that night, our backs turned to each other, both of us hugging the margins of our mattress. And by morning, Norah was feeling fine, and the tension between Mel and me had eased up a bit, like it always does after a night's rest, but we still weren't talking much outside of when I needed help finding Aspen's shoes. My not being willing to pick up Norah from school because I needed to write only fanned the warm coals of the previous night's argument.

HOWEVER, BRINGING HOME THE BACON IS ONLY PART OF THE FATHERHOOD GIG.

Sometimes this happens to me, and I assume it happens to all fathers. It's a problem of focus. I zero in on work and make it the number one priority. I don't do this consciously. And in so many ways, going to work and helping to provide for my family feels like a pat on the back. It feels like I'm really nailing this fatherhood thing. However, bringing home the bacon is only part of the fatherhood gig.

All too often I get caught up in what I need to do for my full-time job (program planning, scheduling student workers, committee meetings), and wherever there are gaps, I cram in my writing obligations (finish my book, freelance writing, blogging), so caring for my own children comes a little too far down the line.

It feels less important.

And when I think about that, I feel guilty. I feel like my understanding of marriage, family and partnership is out of alignment, and for the first time Mel had called me on it.

I finished getting Aspen dressed, got her some toast and set her at the table with the iPad. Norah was in her room with the door shut, doing this half-real, half-fake, overly dramatic crying thing that she often does when she wants attention. And Mel was in the bathroom getting ready. I knew I needed to apologize, but I just couldn't yet.

Everyone left the house, and I was home alone, diligently working on this book and feeling like a jerk.

That afternoon, I picked up Norah from school. She didn't expect me, so she ran across the school gymnasium, brown hair bobbing, to greet me with a big hug. I told her I was sorry. Norah smiled, her two front teeth missing, blue-green eyes open wide, and said, "It's okay." She shrugged like it was no big thing, but the smile on her face told me that it was, in fact, a big thing.

"I love you," I said.

She giggled and hugged me again.

Norah's a pretty forgiving little lady. Somehow

I knew Mel might not be this easy.

That evening we went out to dinner. I made the mistake of letting the kids pick, so we went to McDonald's. As all three kids chomped down on chicken nuggets and played with their new Happy Meal toys, Mel and I worked over some Egg McMuffins.

Behind Mel was a large plastic statue of Ronald McDonald sitting on a bench, his arm across its back. The wall to my right had Big Mac written in large red letters. The table was sticky, and the whole family was sharing one bright-yellow cafeteria tray. It was a weird place to come to a resolution, but this is real life and sometimes the best place to apologize is exactly where you are, even if it's McDonald's.

I gripped her hand and gave her a twisted half smile that felt a lot like an apology. She knew I'd picked up Norah from school, so I didn't need to mention it. I handed her my greasy hash brown in a silent, Napoleon Dynamite show of affection.

She loves hash browns.

I assumed she knew what it all meant.

"Sometimes I just get so caught up in trying to be good at work, that I end up not focusing on what's important . . ."

Before I could say more, she interrupted me with, "It's okay, I get it. I forgive you."

She was chewing on the hash browns as she spoke.

"I'm going to work on it," I said.

"I know," she said.

Then she leaned across the table and brushed some egg from my lip.

WHY MY WIFE STAYS UP LATE

A little after 8:00 a.m. on a Saturday, Mel told me she didn't get enough sleep the night before, and I asked her what time she had gone to bed. All three kids had slept. Mel and I are good about splitting the night, so I'd have known if one of the kids had been up. Aspen got up after 7:30 a.m., which was a good hour and a half later than usual. Generally she's up long before the sun.

I couldn't understand why Mel hadn't had enough sleep unless she stayed up late again, which she probably did.

"A little after 1:00 a.m.," she said. She looked at me with tired red eyes, and I scoffed under my breath and went into lecture mode.

"Why did you stay up that late?" I asked. "I just don't get it. Why didn't you go to bed earlier?"

I went to bed the night before at around 10:00 p.m., as I always do. Ten o'clock rolls around, and pump the brakes, I'm out. Whatever is going on can wait until morning. I just don't care. I want my sleep.

As I left the living room that night, Mel said, "I'll be there in a bit."

But it didn't happen.

I gave her a tight-lipped "I don't have pity for you" face, mostly because this wasn't the first time Mel had stayed up late for, what seemed to me, no good reason.

Ever since we had kids, I'd started to go to bed early. In fact, sleep was my number one priority. Between getting up in the night with children and working two jobs, I never knew when sleep would happen, so I jumped on every sleep opportunity I could.

Before kids, I'd put off sleep to watch a movie. I'd stay up late to hang out with friends for no other reason but to stay up late and be with friends. But after kids, forget about it. There is serious inconsistency when it comes to sleep. I never know when I will be up late cursing and cleaning sheets because Norah drank too much water before going to bed, despite me asking her not to and warning her that she'd wet the bed, all while she gulped down water and stared at me with a jerk face. She sleeps on the top bunk. I mean, honestly, employers who list "can handle stressful situations" as a requirement should observe applicants changing sheets on the top bunk at 2:00 a.m.

On the flip side, I might also be up way too early simply because Aspen wanted to watch *Blue's Clues* at 4:00 a.m., something that had become a common and maddening practice. Steve and Blue had taken over my nightmares. Or maybe Tristan might have a nightmare, so I'd be crammed in the corner of his clutter-covered bed, trying to keep him calm, the extra body heat making me sticky with sweat, his morning breath steaming into my nose. Sometimes he kicked and punched in his sleep, so the next morning felt like the day after a bar fight.

ASPEN WANTED TO WATCH BLUE'S CLUES AT 4:00 A.M., SOMETHING THAT HAD BECOME A COMMON AND MADDENING PRACTICE. STEVE AND BLUE HAD TAKEN OVER MY NIGHTMARES.

It's the inconsistency of sleep as a parent that makes me want to snatch every sleep opportunity. It doesn't take much for me to be out, either. All I ask for is a cool spot on the floor that isn't covered in Cheerios.

Mel was getting up in the night, same as me, so it's odd that she'd refuse to take sleep whenever it was offered to her. But for some reason, Mel always stayed up late, milling around the house, doing who knows what. Maybe she was a double agent, similar to Arnold Schwarzenegger and Jamie Lee Curtis in *True Lies*, and the fate of the nation was in her hands between the hours of 10:00 p.m. and 1:00 a.m. I know that sounds crazy, but in my mind, national security was the only justifiable reason for her to stay up as a parent of small children.

We'd gotten to the point where we never went to bed at the same time. And while that bothered me because I missed us falling asleep together, what bothered me the most was how she stayed up late doing heaven knows what, and then the next day complained about not getting enough sleep. In so many ways, she reminded me of my teenage self, burning the candle at both ends for no good reason.

Mel didn't answer my question about why she'd stayed up so late the night before, and I wondered if it was because she didn't get it either. She was still in her pajamas, her brown hair in a loose ponytail. Our kids were eating breakfast.

She sat down on the sofa, crossed her legs and thought. I sat next to her. I was about to poke at it some more because I was tired of her complaining about sleep, and I wanted her to commit to going to bed at a decent time, when she said, "I spend all day with the kids. All day. And when the kids aren't around, I'm with you—which is great—but when I'm not with you, I'm with the kids. I just . . ." She thought for a moment.

I leaned back into the sofa.

I didn't understand where she was going with all this.

Mel let out a breath, and I couldn't tell if she was irritated or just struggling to describe something she'd never given language to.

"You go to work and you get to be alone in your office. You get your commute in the car to listen to whatever you want on the radio. You get to talk to people who are not your family."

She went on about how I can take a break and be alone. I can step away, while she only has the kids and me. How boogery, drooly, pukey children tugging at her body all day makes her want to crawl inside a bubble.

"Sometimes I want to sit on the sofa and *not* have someone climb on me," she said. "I want to *not* be touched for a while. Sometimes, when the kids are around me all day, clinging to my body, it feels like sensory overload. I just need some me time. Some time that isn't kids and isn't you, and makes me feel like I'm something other than only a mother and a wife."

She paused.

The children laughed at something in the dining room.

"I want some time when the house is quiet and no one is screaming . . ." She raised her eyebrows and said something that really gave me pause.

I JUST NEED SOME ME TIME. SOME TIME THAT ISN'T KIDS AND ISN'T YOU, AND MAKES ME FEEL LIKE I'M SOMETHING OTHER THAN ONLY A MOTHER AND A WIFE.

"Late at night is the only time I get to feel like I did before I was a mother."

Never in our marriage had I thought this was an issue. I assumed Mel loved being a mother.

I'll be honest, I got nervous then.

"Do you not like being a mother?" I asked.

Mel gave a soft half grin. "I love the kids, but this has nothing to do with being a mother. It has everything to do with simply being alone. I don't even want you around sometimes."

My eyes opened wide, and she put her hand on my knee. "I just want time where no one is asking anything of me. Not even you. Right now, that's more important than sleep. Does that make sense?" she asked.

"No," I said.

I paused.

"I mean, it's not something that I need, but I can respect what you are saying."

Mel crawled into the hook of my arm and rested on my shoulder. I put my arm around her, and we just stayed like that for a while, not speaking.

"So are you going to stay up late again tonight?" I asked.

She nodded.

"And then I get to listen to you complain the next day about not getting enough sleep?"

She nodded.

"But there's a reason for it, so I probably shouldn't comment."

"That would be nice," she said.

DAD BOD. MOM BOD.
SEXY BOD.

I posted a selfie of myself heading to the pool with the kids on my Facebook blog page. The caption read, "On our way to the pool! Let's hope this dad bod thing is still popular because I'm going topless." In the background was Norah smiling brightly in a pink bathing suit with yellow goggles on her head. In the car seat was Aspen sleeping soundly. And hiding from the camera was Tristan, who, for the most part, was about as easy to get on film as the Sasquatch.

For those who missed out on the 2015 trend, the term *dad bod* became an Internet hit when nineteen-year-old Clemson sophomore Mackenzie Pearson penned a story in the Clemson *Odyssey* titled "Why

Girls Love the Dad Bod." She suggested that women are more attracted to men whose physiques reflect "a nice balance between a beer gut and working out" than they are to hunks with washboard abs. Suddenly the idea took off, leaving men feeling like they can finally give up on crunches (as if I did crunches), and leaving women to wonder why there is no mom bod.

Case in point: Moments after I posted my selfie, one of my followers commented, "I wish the mom bod was a thing."

Ironically, I was in a Target parking lot, all three kids ready to swim in the back seat, waiting for Mel to pick out a new bathing suit because her old one didn't fit the way it used to after she had our third child.

We argued for quite a while before leaving the house. I told her that she looked sexy in her bathing suit, and she kept coming back at me with retorts as to how having children had ruined her waistline and made her butt fill all the wrong sections of her suit bottoms, while leaving the right sections empty.

She eventually returned back to the van with two swimming suits rather than one, telling me that she couldn't decide which one looked better so she bought both because we were short on time.

"You will look amazing in both," I said.

Then I winked.

Twice.

Mel gave me that sideways look she often gives when she knows I'm being sweet, but she ultimately doesn't believe me. I call this the marriage compliment zone. This is where I give Mel a legitimate compliment, but she doesn't believe me because she feels like I'm obligated to tell her she's sexy. But on the flip side, if I were to say nothing, she'd be angry with me for not complimenting her. Basically, the compliment zone is a no-win situation.

MEL GAVE ME THAT SIDEWAYS LOOK SHE OFTEN GIVES WHEN SHE KNOWS I'M BEING SWEET, BUT SHE ULTIMATELY DOESN'T BELIEVE ME. I CALL THIS THE MARRIAGE COMPLIMENT ZONE.

Not that I'm innocent, or anything. Mel compliments me all the time, and I give her the same look she gave me in the van. All of it is a black hole of insecurity.

Although, I probably should admit that I might be responsible for some of her insecurities. Not that I've ever told my wife that she wasn't attractive. It's more that there was a time before children that I, like many men, viewed mothers as the complete opposite of sexy. When I looked at mothers in bathing suits I often thought, *She fills out all the wrong places, leaving the right places empty.*

There's a water park on the east side of Provo, Utah, the city I grew up in. I spent a lot of time there in the summers. As a teen, I remember thinking that there were always hot girls and . . . moms at the water park. Then, in my twenties, I stopped going because everyone there was either a young girl or a mom.

"What's the point?" I thought.

Obviously I wasn't too interested in the swimming, but let's not linger on that, okay? Thanks.

Just after my 30th birthday, I went back home to visit family, and we ended up at that same old water park. I looked around and thought, *There are some really hot moms here.* Now I'm not telling you this because I want to cheat on my wife. Far from it. It's more that I want to express that something changed in me after being with a mother, and suddenly all those moms looked like dedicated, wonderful women with a surprising amount of sex appeal. And when I think about that, I'm not sure why I never saw it before.

After Target, we went to a community recreation center with a large kid pool and one big yellow slide. It was the kind of place that the whole family can swim for about ten bucks. Mel and I were in good company. Nothing but young kids and parents.

Mel stepped from the changing room in a black one-piece suit looking stoic and beautiful, her hair pulled back into a braid, our toddler, Aspen, on her hip. She looked like the mother of my children, the woman who I'd been married to for years, the person who I've dedicated my life to, the one who supported me through college and cares for our children with dignity and grace—and yet as Mel approached me while I was putting sunblock on our older two children, she looked a little unsure of herself.

ONE OF THE MORE FRUSTRATING AND DIFFICULT NOTIONS FOR ME TO UNDERSTAND AS A HUSBAND AND FATHER IS THAT MY OPINION OF MEL'S BEAUTY ISN'T THE ONE THAT REALLY MATTERS.

"You look amazing," I said.

She gave me that same half smile she gave me earlier in the van.

One of the more frustrating and difficult notions for me to understand as a husband and father is that my opinion of Mel's beauty isn't the one that really matters. Her opinion of herself is the important one, and even though I regularly tell her she's beautiful, she needs to feel attractive, and that can be hard to do when the world is telling mothers that they just aren't sexy.

It was then that I took my shirt off. This was the first time I'd felt confident enough to take my shirt off at the pool in years, and it had something to do with the dad bod, I will admit, but mostly to do with the fact that I'd recently lost 25 pounds after becoming a vegetarian.

Or perhaps I was a flexitarian.

It doesn't matter.

According to the BMI, I was still about ten pounds overweight, but for a father of three in his early 30s, I felt like maybe, just maybe, I could swim without a shirt.

However, about an hour into our swim, Mel took a photo of me playing with Aspen. I looked at it moments later, thought I looked fat and ended up deleting it.

Then I put my shirt back on.

But I must say, I did have a dad bod. I looked like the kind of guy who used to work out but has let himself go. And when Mel asked why I deleted the photo, I shrugged and said, "I looked fat."

She said, "You looked sexy."

I rolled my eyes and suddenly we'd switched roles, and I couldn't for the life of me understand what she saw sexy about my body.

But maybe that right there was the problem. Perhaps it wasn't about my body anymore.

When Norah was three, I remember hunching over her as she sat on the toilet, a wet wipe in my right hand, staring at the business end of my daughter's poopy butt. I was talking her through how to check and make sure she'd gotten every-thing clean, when I felt Mel watching me from the doorway. I looked over at her, and she smiled at me seductively. It was a half-lip smile that she only gives when I'm doing something incredibly sexy. I smiled back. There was no doubt in my mind that she wanted me.

SO MUCH OF MY SEX APPEAL AT THIS AGE HAS TO DO WITH MY ACTIONS AND MY DEDICATION AND HAS LITTLE TO DO WITH THE SHAPE OF MY BODY.

And yet I was wiping a toddler's butt, probably the least sexy, most irritating thing I can think of. In fact, my main goal in that moment was to teach Norah how to do this herself because getting children to wipe their own butt is the real milestone. I didn't once think that I was being sexy.

But it turns out, I was.

So much of my sex appeal at this age has to do with my actions and my dedication and has little to do with the shape of my body.

This is the dad bod.

This is the mom bod.

This is what I didn't understand in my teens or my twenties.

This is what I got wrong.

If Photoshop could capture how much Mel loves her children, how dedicated she is, all the sacrifices she's made for our family, she would be on the cover of every magazine, because that's the really sexy stuff.

A flat stomach and large breasts just look good on paper.

We left the pool. Once the kids and the bags were in the van, I wrapped Mel in my arms next to the passenger door and said, "You were hands down the sexiest woman at the pool today."

Mel smiled and said, "To you."

"That's all I've got," I said.

"Fine," she said. "You were easily the sexiest guy."

"I don't believe you," I said. "Did you see that dad with the nice abs? I can't compete with that."

"You already do," she said.

She winked at me.

Twice.

I AM THE FOURTH CHILD

Mel and I were at a turtle farm in the Cayman Islands. It was part of a cruise we took to celebrate our eleven-year anniversary. With each stop on the cruise, there were excursions. Mel and I are tourists. We aren't really the kind of people to just shoot off and do our own thing, so we pay for tours. We each take turns picking different excursions, and this one, the turtle farm, was Mel's idea. I had assumed it would suck.

I am not a turtle enthusiast. I don't find turtles cute or cuddly or anything like that. In fact, I don't think much about turtles outside of the *Teenage Mutant Ninja Turtles*, which are very exciting but not real, and far from the reality of a large-shelled reptile floating around in seawater. However, I must admit, that once I actually saw one of those massive and majestic 500-pound creatures, I was blown away. The sun was hot, really hot, and it smelled like sea animals and salt water. The turtles splashed and grunted.

MEL SHRUGGED, BUT SHE ALSO GAVE ME A SUSPICIOUS LOOK, A SIDEWAYS GLANCE THAT SEEMED TO SAY, "DON'T YOU DARE TOUCH THOSE TURTLES."

"These things are amazing," I said.

Mel smiled. "I know!" she said. "See. You can have fun at a turtle farm."

I nodded.

We went from one group of turtles to the next. They were massive. All of them had big shells with square-shaped grooves in them. Their necks were long and creased and slick with water, and they had these big beaklike mouths.

We weren't in America. There wasn't anything between us and the turtles outside of a sign that read, Do Not Touch the Turtles.

"Why can't we touch them?" I asked.

Mel shrugged, but she also gave me a suspicious look, a sideways glance that seemed to say, "Don't you dare touch those turtles."

Right then, our guide, Brandon, a skinny

twenty-something Cayman native with dark skin and hair and a spotty, poor attempt at a mustache said, "These turtles have really powerful jaws." He went on to tell us how they are strong enough to bite through another turtle's shell and that our fingers look a lot like the food they are fed. "One of these turtles could very easily bite through your whole hand, which would be bad for the turtle and very unfortunate for you."

Everyone laughed.

I laughed a little, too, but then I thought about touching a turtle . . . despite his warning.

PERHAPS iT MEANS I AM A FOOL AT HEART, A CHILD OF SORTS, WHO WHEN TOLD NOT TO DO SOMETHING LIKE TOUCH A TURTLE, HAS TO TOUCH THE TURTLE.

One of the turtles swam up to me. It looked so friendly. It looked harmless. I didn't know when else I would have the opportunity to touch a large sea turtle. Clearly this wasn't a life goal, but when face-to-face with one, I couldn't help but want to reach out and touch it. I don't know if this means I have a touch fixation when it comes to turtles. I haven't been around them enough. Perhaps it means I am a fool at heart, a child of sorts, who when told not to do something like touch a turtle, has to touch the turtle. A huge part of the temptation was rebellion. There is something exciting about doing what I'm not supposed to, and although I should have grown out of this sort of thing long ago, I clearly hadn't.

I KNEW, EVENTUALLY, MEL AND I WOULD BE THAT OLDER COUPLE, SHRIVELED AND GREASY WITH MOISTURIZER, SMILING WITH SLENDER YELLOW TEETH AND SPARSE GUMS. I'D BE MAKING HORRIBLE GRANDPA JOKES, AND MEL'D BE WEARING PINK SWEATPANTS THAT HAD BEEN THROWN INTO THE WASH A FEW TOO MANY TIMES.

This isn't to say that I'm as impulsive as I was in my teens. I'm not. But right then, on that trip, I felt in the middle. All around us were young couples on honeymoons and older retired couples. The older couples struggled to get around. I saw them with sun hats on and cameras strapped around their necks sitting on benches and busses. They seemed happy, but they also seemed worn out. The young couples seemed impulsively cool. They drank a lot and then danced and then drank some more. Then they got up in the morning and felt fine.

I knew, eventually, Mel and I would be that older couple, shriveled and greasy with moisturizer.

Smiling with slender yellow teeth and sparse gums. I'd be making horrible grandpa jokes, and Mel'd be wearing pink sweatpants that had been thrown into the wash a few too many times. It was inevitable and very uncool, and I didn't like the idea. All of it made me want to set the clock back a little by doing something stupid and impulsive.

While Mel's back was turned and the guide was walking the group to the next tank, I touched a turtle.

Just its shell.

No biggie.

Nothing to get alarmed about.

I felt confident that I was a good distance from its mouth. I wasn't in any danger. I assumed that its shell wouldn't have much feeling. It was pretty solid. Probably bone of some kind. It couldn't have much more feeling than a fingernail or maybe my brainless skull.

I was wrong.

The turtle reached up with its flipper, swatted at my arm and pulled my hand into its mouth.

I kid you not.

I touched the edge of its beak with my fingertips.

I pulled away, jerking my elbow back, just before the thing clamped down with a snort from its oval, quarter-size nostrils.

It grunted loudly and swam away.

Water splashed.

Mel turned around just in time to see me,

red-faced and terrified, my one hand holding the other to make sure I still had all my digits.

"Really?" she said. "They tell you not to touch the turtle, and what do you do?"

I shrugged.

"You. Touch. It."

She poked me in the chest with each word.

"You're like a child!"

Sadly, this wasn't the first time she'd told me this. Or the second or third . . .

I held up my hand. Rocked it from side to side. Wiggled my fingers. Counted them. "See! I'm good! Nothing happened."

"YOU'RE LIKE A CHILD!" SADLY, THIS WASN'T THE FIRST TIME SHE'D TOLD ME THIS. OR THE SECOND OR THIRD . . .

"What if you'd lost your hand?" she said.

"But I didn't," I said. I held up my hand again. "It's all good."

We stood next to the tank for a while. The tour group had moved off, out of sight. I don't think Mel was mad.

She was worse than that.

She'd gone into a place where no husband ever wants his wife to go.

Disappointment.

She was completely, 100 percent, disappointed in me. I could see it in her fists. I could see it in her stern, soft, pink, straight lips. I could see it as she turned her back to me and folded her arms, shoulders ridged.

In the past I've heard women with three kids jokingly say that they really had four kids (including their husband). This joke always bothered me. I felt it gave good, upstanding husbands and fathers, like myself, a bad rap.

SHE'D GONE INTO A PLACE WHERE NO HUSBAND EVER WANTS HIS WIFE TO GO. DISAPPOINTMENT.

But thinking back on this incident with the sea turtle, I realized that perhaps Mel actually had four kids. Not just three. I cannot fully describe how embarrassed I was. Me, a grown man, father of three, college graduate and mortgage owner. It was a deep, rich shame, frothy and thick and difficult to swallow.

Mel sighed.

We walked to the next part of the turtle exhibit, a large pool with baby turtles. We were allowed to climb in and actually hold the little guys, and as they splashed around, it was difficult to keep arguing. They were the most adorable little black-eyed creatures we'd ever seen.

I took a picture of Mel holding one. She smiled at me, and like a fool, I brought it up again.

"If I lost my hand, would you still love me?"

I was trying to make light of the situation, and it was working to some extent. Mel gave me a half grin. Then she placed the baby turtle back in the water, stood up straight and said, "You were told not to touch the turtle."

She looked at me in silence, letting the cold hard fact sink in. It was the same tone she used the last time my daughter took a face-plant after refusing to tie her shoes.

She told me that if I'd lost my hand, she'd have to explain to everyone, every single person, that her husband was an idiot who somehow managed to lose his hand to a sea turtle.

"I'm not saying that I'd leave you. But I would be so embarrassed, and it would take me some time to get over you doing something so *stupid*."

The conversation reminded me of *Arrested Development*, when Buster Bluth loses his hand during a seal attack. It was funny on the show, but I don't know how funny it would be in real life. I have to assume it would be difficult for Mel to explain that I lost my hand to one of the friendliest sea creatures ever. I'd have probably made trending news on Facebook. I'd have been *that* guy, and, most importantly, Mel would have been married to *that* guy, and no one wants to be married to the dumbass who lost his hand because he just couldn't stop himself from reaching out and touching a sea turtle.

We didn't talk for a while after that unless we had to. We went to a little cabana and ordered lunch. It started raining in big fat tropical drops outside, and we sat there and ate in silence.

I'D HAVE BEEN THAT GUY. AND, MOST IMPORTANTLY, MEL WOULD HAVE BEEN MARRIED TO THAT GUY. AND NO ONE WANTS TO BE MARRIED TO THE DUMBASS WHO LOST HIS HAND BECAUSE HE JUST COULDN'T STOP HIMSELF FROM REACHING OUT AND TOUCHING A SEA TURTLE.

I looked out on the turtle park, watching the rain, and thought back to several years earlier, to the first time Mel said I was like a child. We'd only been married for two years, and I had gotten knocked out riding a snowboard.

I'd dropped that same cliff several times as a single man. I was with a group of unmarried friends, and I wanted to show them how cool I still was, even though I was married now.

A few inches before the drop, the front of my board snagged a small rock. My board stopped, but my body kept moving. I ended up taking a headfirst dive from about fifteen feet up and getting knocked out, ice cold.

I don't know how long I was out, but when I came to, I could hear my buddies calling my name from above. Then I felt a pain in my head.

"Hey!" I said.

"You okay?" one friend asked.

"Yeah, I'm good."

"That was really awesome," he said.

I finished out the day riding despite the dizziness. I didn't want my buddies to know how badly I'd been hurt, because I didn't want them to see me as weak. Thinking back, riding off that cliff was similar to the impulse I had to touch that turtle.

I came home from snowboarding with the intention of not telling Mel. It felt like I didn't want to tell my parents that I had wrecked the car or some other stupid thing I might have done as a teen. I probably wouldn't have said a word to her if I hadn't broken my cell phone in the crash, something I didn't realize until I tried to use it on the drive home.

Mel was in the living room of our small condo. We didn't have kids yet.

"Why didn't you answer my calls?" she asked.

I thought about lying to her. But then I realized that if I was willing to lie about wrecking on my snowboard, who knows what else I was willing to lie about. So I told her what had happened as if it were some funny joke.

"You fell off a cliff and onto your head?" She

was really concerned at first. She asked if I needed a doctor, and I told her no.

Then she got angry and told me that I couldn't snowboard anymore. We argued about that for a while, which seems foolish now considering I haven't been snowboarding since we had kids. Then she said, "I don't understand why hitting your head is cool. It's not cool. It's scary. You're like a child."

I got pretty offended at the time. But that all seemed to stop when her eyes grew misty, and she said, "I'm not going to lose you over something so stupid."

As I thought about that first time she called me a child and compared it to the time with the turtle, I realized that she hadn't meant it as an insult. What she was trying to say was, "I don't want to lose you."

Which really means, "I love you."

We got on the bus to head back to our cruise ship. We still hadn't talked much. I don't think we were really fighting anymore, but we weren't out of the woods yet. Across from us was an older couple, probably in their late 60s. He was in the standard faded blue old-man polo that had seen a few too many wash cycles, with navy slacks and brown SAS-brand shoes, his pant legs high on the calf, and weary brown socks sagging toward his ankles. She had on a pink T-shirt that read *World's*

Greatest Grandmother, along with gray slacks and the same brown SAS-brand shoes her husband was wearing. She lay her gray dome of curls on her husband's shoulder and closed her eyes. It had been a long day. The man smiled and looked down at her. Then he took her hand, and she smiled, her eyes still shut. It was probably one of the sweetest things I'd ever seen.

Mel took my hand and said, "That's what I want for us."

Mel often looks forward to our lives together with excitement, while I tend to look backward and feel like I've lost my coolness and end up doing something stupid.

But right then, we were in sync.

I looked over at Mel and said, "I'm sorry I touched the turtle."

"It's fine," she said. "Please stop doing stupid things, okay?"

"Deal," I said.

Then Mel leaned into my shoulder, and for a moment we looked a lot like the older couple across from us on the bus.

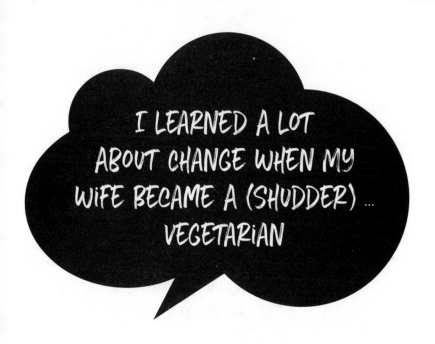

I LEARNED A LOT ABOUT CHANGE WHEN MY WIFE BECAME A (SHUDDER) ... VEGETARIAN

When Mel told me she wanted to be a vegetarian, I almost crapped my pants. I looked her in the eyes and wondered if this was grounds for divorce. I thought about the day I proposed. After she had said yes, we went to Applebee's for steak and potatoes. Anniversaries, birthdays, holidays, graduations, successes and failures—every significant moment in our life together was accompanied by beef, chicken or pork.

Mostly pork.

Bacon is the heroin of meat.

To further complicate things, meat was emotionally significant to me. When I was sixteen, I bought my first barbeque, a large charcoal outfit that came with a side table and instructions on how to smoke a turkey. I'd obtained my driver's license and first car a few weeks earlier, and I recall thinking that the grill was equally significant.

> WE WERE HAVING DINNER WHEN SHE TOLD ME ABOUT HER DECISION TO GIVE UP MEAT. THE SETTING HURT ALMOST AS MUCH AS THE NEWS. IT FELT LIKE SHE'D TOLD ME ABOUT AN AFFAIR WHILE WE WERE HAVING SEX.

Eight years in, Mel was changing the dynamics of our marriage. It felt like she was trying to take away something very important not only to me, but also to my life and our marriage.

We were having dinner when she told me about her decision to give up meat. The setting hurt almost as much as the news. It felt like she'd told me about an affair while we were having sex. I went a little crazy. I asked her a silly question that I already knew the answer to.

"Have you tried meat?"

Mel looked confused. "Well, yeah."

"No. No," I said. I shook my hands in front of me, palms out. "I mean have you put it in your mouth? Because it's really good. Anyone who has tried meat wouldn't make this decision."

Mel rolled her eyes.

We were living in a small, cramped, third-floor apartment at the time. Our table sat in a corner next to the door. It wasn't really a dining room; it was more of the space between the kitchen and the living room. Our two children were at the table. Tristan was six and Norah was four. Tristan looked at me with confused blue eyes and asked, "What is a vegetarian?"

Mel started to answer, but I beat her to it. "It's nothing to worry about," I said. "It's where people only eat fruits and vegetables."

THE MOMENT I SAID ". . . ONLY EAT FRUITS AND VEGETABLES," TRISTAN LOOKED AT ME WITH PUCKERED LIPS LIKE I WAS DESCRIBING SAVAGES.

I wanted to add that they had no soul or understanding of joy. I wanted to tell him that they were miserable people who didn't eat Happy Meals. But I didn't need to. The moment I said ". . . only eat fruits and vegetables," Tristan looked at me with puckered lips like I was describing savages.

"I'm *not* a vegetarian," he said.

"That's right, son" I said.

I looked Mel straight in the eyes, "That's right."

"The doctor told me that if I eat less meat, I would have less back pain," she said. "So I stopped eating so much meat. Now meat makes me feel sick."

I have to admit, what she said sounded reasonable. However, I was beyond reason. Frankly, I was frightened.

Then she told me about the documentary *Forks Over Knives*. "It was on Netflix," she said. Apparently, it showed that most, if not all, of the degenerative diseases that afflict us can be controlled or even reversed by not eating animal-based foods. She started talking about how healthy a low-fat, whole-food, plant-based diet was, and I tried to wrap my head around these new terms, none of which sounded appetizing.

Then she told me about other documentaries that showed the brutality of the food industry. She talked about sad and abused animals, chickens that could hardly walk living in heaping piles of their own crap, sad and abused pigs, cows being fed corn mixed with steroids rather than hay.

What she described sounded very different from my grandfather's farm. He was a beef farmer, and he treated the animals humanely. He never pumped them full of steroids and antibiotics. Only hay. For the most part, they seemed to live normal cow lives, wandering about, grazing and pooping. Suddenly, we had very different images of how meat was produced and what it meant. Meat made me think of tractor rides with my grandfather, grilling with my friends, mornings with my father and proposing to my wife, whereas it now made

Mel think about cows being filled with hormones and then trapped in a pen, something similar to how Wolverine was created in the *X-Men*.

I got scared and said, "Let's cook some sausage and forget about all of this."

She didn't laugh. I knew she was serious.

WHEN WE GOT MARRIED, SHE WAS A MEAT EATER, AND I LIKED THAT ABOUT HER. NOW SHE WASN'T GOING TO BE A MEAT EATER, AND IT FELT LIKE SHE WAS CHANGING IN A WAY I WASN'T COMFORTABLE WITH.

The whole situation reminded me of a line in *Pulp Fiction* where Jules (Samuel L. Jackson) says, ". . . my girlfriend's a vegetarian, which pretty much makes me a vegetarian." After being married for a few years, I knew this would be the case. Mel and I had been together long enough for me to understand that if she did, actually, make this life change, I would wind up changing with her. And while I loved meat, I think what really bothered me about her becoming a vegetarian was that it felt like she was changing our contract. When we got married, she was a meat eater, and I liked that about her. Now she wasn't going to be a meat eater, and it felt like she was changing in a way I wasn't comfortable with.

I took a deep breath, and I thought about how difficult it would be for Mel to stick to this diet. We had meat with nearly every meal. This would be a huge shift in her life. I really doubted she could stick with it.

Mel broke the silence. "How about you do it with me?"

I laughed.

"There's no way," I said.

"You might change your mind if you watched *Forks Over Knives*," she said. "It's really moving. I want you to watch it with me."

"Are you crazy?" I asked. "Look what it did to you! No. I'd rather not."

Mel gave me the heartstrings look.

Her blue eyes got a little soft as she tucked in her small, slender lower lip. She only makes this face when I'm being a jerk. I thought about her supporting my return to college. I thought about how she let me do a study abroad program in London when Tristan was only one year old.

"Fine. OK. I'm sorry. If this is what you want, I will support you."

Which was only half true. When she ate like a vegetarian, I ate like a vegetarian. But I will admit, I tried hard to tempt her. I often began conversations with, "It's too bad you are a vegetarian because . . ." and then I'd go on to describe amazing meat-filled lunches I'd had with my coworkers. "We went to this Mexican place and the chicken taco tasted like it was seasoned by a God!" Or, "The burger I ate for lunch had three patties. It was three times as delicious as a regular burger." Or, "They opened a Buffalo Wild Wings next to the university. You would have loved the new sauces. But . . . you know . . ." I always held a tone of remorse, almost like I was talking about someone who'd died. This was not something intentional; it just came out that way. And, I suppose, it felt that way, too.

SHE WAS BECOMING SOMEONE DIFFERENT. AND I WAS FACED WITH THE DECISION TO ACCEPT HER CHANGE AND CONTINUE TO LOVE HER OR TO FIGHT IT AND TRY TO MAKE HER REMAIN SOMEONE SHE DIDN'T WANT TO BE ANYMORE.

When I think back on this moment, it feels like I was trying to force her to forever be the meat-eating person I had fallen in love with. But she was becoming someone different, and I was faced with the decision to accept her change and continue to love her or to fight it and try to make her remain someone she didn't want to be anymore.

When Mel and I got married, I assumed she'd be that same person forever, but that really wasn't the case. Not that she suddenly wanted an open marriage or anything; it's more that growing up doesn't end in your teens. I used to jokingly tell friends that the reality of long-term commitment is looking at your spouse and imagining them with gray hair and an extra 30 pounds. Now, after being married for over a decade, I can confidently say that it's much more complicated than that. It means looking at Mel and imagining her changing religions or taking up knitting or deciding to run a marathon or learning to play the piano even if she has no musical talent or becoming a *freaking* vegetarian.

I EVEN ONCE WROTE, "I LOVE YOU" IN STRIPS OF BACON ON THE COUNTER.

Six months after Mel gave up meat, I started to regularly cook bacon the way she liked it best—slowly cooked, crispy and golden brown. It was easy for the smell of bacon to drift into every room of our small apartment.

I even once wrote, "I love you" in strips of bacon on the counter.

It was petty.

One evening as I was making bacon and eggs, Mel walked into the kitchen and said, "That smells really good."

I smiled at her and held the plate out to her. I felt sinister, evil, capable of doing anything. I looked her in the eyes as she reached for a strip of bacon, and I smiled slyly, a devil's grin, and thought about the moment in the Bible when Eve took the apple, *Your eyes will be opened as soon as you eat it, and you will be like God, knowing both good and evil.*

Mel took a strip of bacon and popped it in her mouth. And as she did, I opened my mouth and my eyes. My face seemed to say, *Got ya!* But I didn't say it. Nor did I point at the bacon and remind her that she was a vegetarian. I held my comments, hopeful that she'd take another strip. And she did. Mel chewed slowly, savoring the moment. Perhaps it's because it'd been awhile, but she looked so sexy.

She gave me a crooked sinful smile, and I got really excited.

I assumed it was over.

She ate bacon a few more times over the next few days, munching it down slyly, and the satisfaction on her face gave me hope that we could go back to our normal meat-eating lives. But it never happened. The only meat I ever saw her eat was bacon.

One evening, as she was in our small kitchen preparing a quinoa and black bean casserole, I said, "Vegetarians don't eat bacon. You know that . . . right? Don't you think it is time to stop living a lie?"

Mel turned and placed her hand on her hip. This is a stance that she gives me only when I have said something outrageously incorrect, and she is going to savor the opportunity to set me straight.

"Maybe I'm not a vegetarian anymore," she said. She paused for a moment, and my heart leaped.

"I've decided to be a flexitarian." She raised her eyebrows, and I placed my face in my hands.

"What's a flexitarian?" I asked through my fingers.

She told me that it is semivegetarianism, and it means that she can have a little meat. We went back and forth for a bit, me listing cuts of meat and her telling me that she still won't eat them. Eventually we narrowed down the list.

"I will eat bacon, sometimes."

"Obviously," I said.

"And I will have ham or turkey on Christmas and Thanksgiving."

She stopped there. I thought of all the additional possibilities. I thought about all the other options she had. I thought about the fact that her head kind of looked like a burger, and I had to pause and wonder if I was going through meat withdrawals of some kind.

"That's it?" I asked.

She nodded.

In my head, I called her a hypocrite. I thought about how she needed to be black and white on this. She either was or she wasn't. But then a crazy thing happened. The more I thought about it, the more reasonable it sounded. She was really living within her restrictions and only bending her standards occasionally. And I hated that I thought that way. I hated that the way she was sticking to her guns was making me respect her more.

"Listen," she said. "You've been a real jerk about me becoming a vegetarian. I made this change because I thought it would be good for me. I wish you'd trust me."

She went into the bedroom and shut the door.

It was the "trust me" part that gave me pause. I never thought about it that way. I needed to trust her to make good decisions. This whole time I was a little too worried about myself.

We didn't have some amazing makeup discussion. I told her I was sorry, and we stopped arguing.

I dropped it, which led to me starting to accept it, and about a year later, I found myself sitting across from Mel at the dinner table eating a black bean quinoa burrito bowl with kiwis on the side. Not a scrap of meat at the table.

We now lived in a house. Naturally our children were there, too, although they weren't all that interested in what we were eating, especially Tristan. His arms were folded on the table; his chin resting on them.

"You need to get some pants that fit," Mel said.

As predicted, I became a vegetarian. Or perhaps I'm a flexitarian. I don't know. Regardless, I lost almost 25 pounds and most of my clothing hung from me. I smiled at her and asked that she pass the black beans.

Beneath the table, Tristan tapped my foot with his. He looked up at me, and I leaned down. "Can

I have some dinosaur chicken?" he whispered. He was talking about dinosaur-shaped chicken nuggets from the freezer, his favorite meal, second only to mac and cheese.

"I don't like that," he pointed at the food on the table and spoke with the utmost sincerity, his eyebrows in full arch as though our very fine meal was actually a hate crime.

"Have you tried it?" I asked.

Tristan shook his head, "I don't like fruits and vegetables."

"I didn't either until recently. But your mom does. And you know what?"

"What?" he said.

"We need to trust her to make good decisions for herself and for us," I said.

I wanted to tell him about how I lost weight by eating fruits and vegetables. I wanted to mention how I didn't want to eat this way, but now that I do, it's been great for my health. I wanted to tell him that sometimes people in our lives change, and if it's a good change, we need to change with them because it will only make us better. But I didn't know if he'd get all that, so instead I made a deal with him. I told him that if he ate two slices of kiwi and half of his bowl, I'd make him three chicken nuggets, half a portion.

He said no at first.

"Sometimes you have to try new things even if you don't like them. And do you know what happens?"

"What?" he said.

"You start to like them."

I poked his side, and he rolled his eyes. Then he reluctantly agreed.

Mel smiled at me from across the table.

CHILL, DUDE.
SHE'S JUST VENTING.

I was at work on a Sunday when I got a text from Mel, "I've officially lost it today."

I had gone to work early that morning and would be there until late. Before that message, I got one that read, "Church was just great today." She was being sarcastic. It was the rolling eyes emoji that gave her away.

Mel, being the hard-core mom that she is, took all three kids (at the time, ages one, six and eight) to church by herself. I've done this before, so I know that sitting on a church bench with those three little nutjobs feels like being trapped in a hot cage with wild animals wearing a suit and dresses, their little teeth spackled with saltine crackers.

"I'm hot."

"I'm bored."

"I need to poop."

Times a bazillion.

I KNOW THAT SITTING ON A CHURCH BENCH WITH THOSE THREE LITTLE NUTJOBS FEELS LIKE BEING TRAPPED IN A HOT CAGE WITH WILD ANIMALS WEARING A SUIT AND DRESSES, THEIR LITTLE TEETH SPACKLED WITH SALTINE CRACKERS.

That morning she had sent a picture of Norah in a blue-and-white Queen Elsa play dress, sitting on the living room floor screaming, butt up in the air, feet and head down, almost as if she were in some angry Disney princess–themed yoga pose.

I sent back, "I've heard about goat yoga and wine yoga, but angry princess yoga is new to me."

I thought I was funny.

Turns out I'm not.

She texted back, "Not in the mood," along with a red angry-faced emoji.

I'm sure the whole day, from getting the children up, to getting them to church, to sitting through church, was hell. To make matters worse, we're

Mormons, which means church lasts for three hours.

I kid you not.

I once read online that three hours of church with three kids under ten is comparable to competing in an Ironman.

(Please don't tell my bishop I wrote that.)

> # I ONCE READ ONLINE THAT THREE HOURS OF CHURCH WITH THREE KIDS UNDER TEN IS COMPARABLE TO COMPETING IN AN IRONMAN .... (PLEASE DON'T TELL MY BISHOP I WROTE THAT.)

I'd been putting in a lot of hours at work. I worked for the athletics department at a university, and during the summer I managed summer bridge programs. These were programs that help students straight out of high school make the transition to college. They take hours of planning and programming. There was also the fact that some of my student athletes viewed college classes like I might view a part-time coffee shop job. They just weren't that invested, and my job over the summer was to get them invested. Let's just say I was pretty popular.

I'd been working weekends and evenings, and when I was home, I wasn't really there. I was stuck on my phone, answering text messages from student workers.

It was a new job, and Mel and I are were both adjusting to it, which meant I got a lot of messages like the one above from Mel.

The crazy thing is, I always referred to it as "my new job." I talked a lot about my new responsibilities and stresses, but, honestly, were it not for Mel caring for our children during the day, there's no way I could've taken a job with such a crazy schedule. So it really was our new job. When I worked evenings, Mel worked evenings. When I worked weekends, Mel worked weekends.

Naturally, I didn't think about any of that when I got Mel's text.

I never do.

I thought about the stress of my new job and felt a pressure in my chest, a tenseness that I couldn't really define, so I stopped making jokes, and I got angry. I thought, "I have got so much going on. I don't need this."

I felt the tug-of-war between work and home.

As a father, I feel this every time I miss a soccer game for a late-night work meeting, or I miss a parent-teacher conference because it happens during the day, or when I can't make it home for dinner. I wanted to be home, spending time with my family, but I also felt a tremendous responsibility to support my family and be successful.

I looked at Mel's text, and I felt the pressure all the more.

I wanted to call her and tell her I was frustrated

at work and that I wished I could be there. I wanted to tell her I was sorry. I wanted her to tell me a few good things that happened so I could feel better. I wanted to call and fix her problems. But I knew none of that would change a thing.

I was stuck at work.

She was stuck at home.

THERE IS A DIFFERENCE BETWEEN VENTING AND COMPLAINING.

So I paused for a moment. I considered what she might actually be saying.

Thinking back, Mel's intention wasn't to make me feel bad. She wasn't complaining, either.

She was venting.

This is something that took me a long time to understand.

There is a difference between venting and complaining. Complaining is asking for change. When Mel complains, she wants me to present her with an alternative. Venting is getting it off your chest. This is where Mel just wants me to listen to her frustrations. This is the same as when I come home and complain about students I work with. I don't expect Mel to solve the problem (although sometimes she does help me think through a situation).

What I want is for her to listen and understand.

It was in that moment that I did something I

almost never do. I realized that maybe, just maybe, I was overreacting.

I know . . . pump the brakes. I'm admitting it.

"I'm sorry," I sent back. "I love you. We can talk about it tonight when I get home, if you'd like."

"I love you, too," she wrote. "I'm just venting. Yes, let's talk. That would be nice."

SORRY TO BREAK IT
TO YOU, BUT SEX ISN'T
AN OBLIGATION

It was around 9:30 p.m. on a Tuesday. Tristan and Norah were in bed, and Mel was feeding baby Aspen on the sofa. I was sitting across from her in an easy chair, leaning down to fill my gym bag for the following day. Moments earlier I'd been messing around online and came across a story in the *Huffington Post* about a guy making a spreadsheet to track all the times he'd been turned down for sex by his wife. The spreadsheet was originally posted on Reddit, and online commenters had a field day.

I asked Mel if she'd seen the story, and she said she hadn't, so I told her about it. She didn't scoff, like this guy was pathetic. And she didn't get angry and say that this man was a real lowlife.

Instead she said, "That's really sad."

And like Mel, I couldn't help but feel sorry for this marriage.

Many of the comments were people lashing out at this man's crappy attempt to communicate to his wife about something he viewed as a problem in their marriage. Maybe he assumed that if she saw things visually it would help fix the problem, but instead he was trying to fix his marriage like he would a struggling investment. A lack of sex and his misunderstandings of how to discuss issues with his wife were simply the tip of the iceberg.

"You know . . . after being married for a while, this story really hit home," I said.

I ONCE READ THAT THE THREE BIGGEST CAUSES OF DIVORCE WERE RELIGION, MONEY AND SEX.

Mel gave me a wide-eyed, curious look. Then she folded her arms as though she were waiting for this conversation to go off the rails and into another discussion about sexual frequency. Then she twisted her lips to the side, and asked, "You're not going to show me a spreadsheet, are you?"

Frequency of sex was something we'd struggled with in our marriage. I once read that the three biggest causes of divorce were religion, money and sex. We've always been pretty good with the first two, but the latter ... well ... that's a different story.

Sometimes we've been consistent, and other times we've gone long stretches with little more than a quick kiss in the kitchen. I think a lot of marriages have this same problem, particularly when there are small kids in the home, but that doesn't make it any less frustrating.

Honestly, we've fought about sex more than anything else during our marriage. Having children didn't help. Not. At. All.

A big part of the problem was me.

When we first got married, I expected sex. I assumed it was owed to me, like "you are obligated to have sex with your husband whenever he feels the need" was listed on our wedding certificate.

I held to that assumption for years.

HONESTLY, WE'VE FOUGHT ABOUT SEX MORE THAN ANYTHING ELSE DURING OUR MARRIAGE.

When Tristan was one year old, I remember Mel putting him down late at night. We'd had three horrible up-all-night-with-a-screaming-baby nights with that boy. Mel's eyes were bloodshot, her hair was greasy and spit-up was on her T-shirt. She hadn't had a chance to shower in a couple of days because motherhood sucks that way.

Like an idiot, I assumed this was the perfect time to ask for sex.

"We don't have anything else going on." I said. "Why not? Tristan's asleep. What's the problem?"

"Seriously?" Mel said. Her hands hung limply at her sides, her shoulders sagged, her eyes were half shut, everything about her said *exhausted*.

"You don't have anything else going on. You don't. I'm exhausted, and I'd like a shower, and I'm not in the mood. Not even a little bit."

Thinking back on this moment, what Mel said was totally reasonable. But that didn't seem to work for me. I pushed the subject.

That's when we started arguing.

I slept on the sofa that night. At the time I felt cheated and I couldn't understand how I'd crossed a line. This story shouldn't surprise anyone who's been married for a few years.

I can't count how many times I've leaned in for a kiss while Mel was busy cleaning or looking over bills or getting ready to go to bed after a long night or exhausted from wrangling kids and asked for sex.

We didn't always argue when she said "not now," but I always felt picked on.

Considering all of the above, I wasn't all that surprised when Mel asked if I was going to show her a spreadsheet of my own sexual grievances. Although we'd gotten better at communicating and compromising over the years, it had only been recently that I'd started to stop thinking of sex as an obligation, and this story about the spreadsheet felt like a mile marker showing me how far I'd come. In fact, a few years earlier, I had written an article about my frustrations with sex and marriage in the *Good Men Project*, and online commenters schooled me. Or should I say, skewered me?

Either way, it was an eye-opening experience.

I laughed softly and said, "No. It's just that . . . for a long time I made the assumption that sex was something I was owed. Something that you were obligated to give me, and if you didn't, then you were doing something wrong. I think this spreadsheet guy had the same problem."

I paused for a moment, let out a deep breath, and continued. "In fact, there was a time early in our marriage, just after we had Tristan, that I thought about making a list of all the times you said "no."

"I feel horrible about this."

"This guy turned marriage into a checklist." I paused for a moment and collected my thoughts. "I guess what I'm saying is, I want us to have something rooted in love, not a checklist. I want you to want to have sex with me, not feel like it's something you have to do."

I got up and sat beside her on the sofa. "My question now is, how can I woo you more?"

I started to say more, but Mel smiled and put up her hand.

She thought for a moment, breathed in through her nose and twisted her lips with thought.

Then she said, "It's not you. I don't think there is anything more you can do. Or at least I'm not going to ask you to do anything more. You do a lot. You work two jobs. You pitch in. You're a good dad, and I love you. It's not that I don't want to have sex with you. There is just so much in the way."

She went on, telling me some of the details of her busy life, caring for the new baby, chores and so on. At the time she was working on a degree, so she threw classwork on the pile, too.

"What bothers me the most about every time we talk about sex is that you make it out like I am the problem," she said. "I'm not stopping it because I don't love you, and it's not because you don't do enough or that you are not attractive. I am not the problem. I want to have sex. You are not the problem. Life is the problem. You don't need to make me a spreadsheet for me to know that we don't have as much sex as we did before having kids. I know that. It bugs me, too. And if you did make one, all it would prove is that we have crazy busy lives."

What she said hit home. I realized how stupid I had been.

"I'm sorry," I said. "I didn't mean to make you out to be the problem. I'm just frustrated with the situation, I guess."

"Me, too," she said.

"I'M GLAD YOU GET IT," SHE SAID. "BECAUSE I'M EXHAUSTED, AND IT'S TOO LATE FOR SEX."

I leaned over and kissed Mel, and it seemed fitting that our new baby was still in her arms between us.

"OK," I said. "I get it. I don't love it. But I get it."

I kissed her lips, and then I kissed her neck. I assumed we were making up.

"I'm glad you get it," she said. "Because I'm exhausted, and it's too late for sex."

THERE ARE THINGS
I DO THAT MAKE ME
LESS ATTRACTIVE

I was attempting to get Mel up for church, but it wasn't going well. I tapped her shoulder and said something like, "Good morning, starshine." She grunted, rolled over, and said, "You were snoring again. I hardly slept."

She was angry, I could tell, but she was trying to keep calm because she knew that it wasn't something I could control. This didn't exactly lead to an argument. It led to something between an argument and a discussion, a void of space that we commonly find ourselves in. Mel wants to tell me how she's really feeling but doesn't, so I end up making stupid jokes hoping to ease the tension, only making it worse, which along with snoring I have to assume is an unattractive quality.

"I don't snore," I said. "You don't have any proof."

I'd been up for a while with our kids. Despite Mel sleeping in later than I did, she had the red eyes of someone who'd stayed up all night.

AT FIRST IT SOUNDED LIKE A CHAINSAW ATTACKING A WILD BEAR, THEN IT SHIFTED TO AN ASTHMATIC DARTH VADER, THEN A BITTERLY DISAPPOINTED GOAT AND FINISHED WITH A HORSE EATING AN EXTRA-JUICY APPLE.

She reached to the floor beside our bed and snagged her phone. She rolled over, the phone close to her face because she wasn't wearing her glasses, tapped the screen a few times, and then a deep unsettling sound came through. At first it sounded like a chainsaw attacking a wild bear, then it shifted to an asthmatic Darth Vader, then a bitterly disappointed goat and finished with a horse eating an extra-juicy apple.

In the past, I'd used this same argument of no evidence when she complained about my snoring. "You can't prove it." And while I always said it jokingly, I honestly didn't want to believe that I'd reached this stage. When I was a Boy Scout, I had a scoutmaster who sounded like a tornado destroying a symphony. Thinking back, he was probably in his late 30s at the time, only a few years older than I was during this conversation.

I recall setting up my tent as far away from him as possible and still struggling to sleep. One night while camping, I lay awake and thought about how irritating he was. I thought about how I wanted to take my dirty socks, the ones I'd worn hiking all day, and cram them in his stupid trumpet mouth. I wanted to stuff a few bars of soap in my pillowcase and beat him silent.

When Mel first mentioned my snoring a couple of years earlier, all I could think about was that scoutmaster, how old I thought he seemed because he snored, and how it was evidence that I was becoming him. So I denied it. Playfully, but it was still denial. While I often challenged her to give me evidence of my snoring, I never actually thought she'd *do it*. Nor did I think that the sounds coming from my body in the night could possibly be that irritating.

While listening to the recording, I couldn't help but imagine Mel half-awake in the night, her eyes twisted in sleep-deprived rage, leaning into my face with a phone to get that recording of me snoring next to her.

I wanted to keep denying it. I wanted to tell Mel that there was no way on earth that was me. Perhaps it was some recording she found online.

Then I wondered if Mel ever thought about

beating me in the night with a pillowcase full of soap.

"How do you still love me?" I asked.

THEN I WONDERED iF MEL EVER THOUGHT ABOUT BEATING ME iN THE NiGHT WiTH A PiLLOWCASE FULL OF SOAP.

Mel sat up in bed. Despite it being late spring, she was in green pajama pants with Christmas trees on them and a long-sleeved brown shirt. They were her comfort clothes, although she didn't seem all that comfortable at the moment. She seemed a little tense because I don't think she anticipated my question. In the past, our conversations about snoring revolved around me seeing a doctor, which I'd done. All of it boiled down to me losing some weight. I'd done that, too. In fact, I'd tried a few things. Nothing worked.

I still snored.

But this time our conversation went in a different direction.

"Why do you ask?" she said.

"Because that's the most unsexy sound I've ever heard," I said. I wanted to tell her about my scoutmaster but didn't. I didn't want her to know about him because I was afraid it would somehow confirm that I was becoming this old, balding, snoring man, which I didn't want to be.

Mel thought about what I said for a moment. Then she laughed.

"This isn't funny," I said. "Why are you laughing?"

"I don't know," she said. "I just . . . there are a lot of things that you do that are unattractive. But I still love you."

She smiled at me.

I did not smile back.

"Like what?" I said

"Well . . . there's all the boogers collecting below the driver's seat in your car."

I froze.

I didn't know she knew about that. I always thought I'd been pretty discreet with my booger picking, but clearly . . . it was out!

She went on. She mentioned the skid marks in my underwear, how I sometimes poop with the door open, how I sometimes fart in the van and then open *all* the windows and turn on the air and wink at her as if I'm being courteous, but I'm just being nasty, how whenever we go to the Never Ending Pasta Bowl at the Olive Garden I always eat like six bowls of pasta and act like it's an accomplishment, but it's actually pretty gross.

"Do you want me to continue?" she said.

I knew about this stuff, but I'd never had it all laid out before me. And some of it I didn't even think was an issue, like the pasta thing.

"Holy crap," I said. "No, please stop talking."

I'll admit, I was offended. Or maybe I was embarrassed. It was a probably a mix of both.

"I'm sorry," Mel said. She closed her eyes. "I'm just really tired. I didn't mean to say all that."

We sat in silence for a while.

"I still love you," she said. "It's just . . . we've just been together for a while, and I've noticed some things."

There was a part of me, back in my twenties, when I assumed that Mel would always find me sexy. I'm not sure where this assumption came from, but as I've gotten older, I've started to realize that isn't the case. That there are things that I do that make me less attractive. Some of them I can control. Picking my nose for example. I need to grow out of that nasty little habit. And pooping with the door open is just me being lazy. But the ones that are difficult to control, the ones that just come with age, like snoring and the way gravity is starting to pull my body into a lopsided mess, I really struggle with. I think everyone does. It's just the reality of getting older.

"Yeah, but why?" I said. "All that stuff you listed should be grounds for divorce. No judge in the world would blame you for leaving me once they saw my booger collection."

Mel didn't exactly agree with me, but she didn't exactly disagree. She looked down at her phone.

"You're the one that kept asking for evidence," she said.

I didn't respond.

"Listen, you're wrong," she said. "I'm not going to leave you because you snore. Or any of that other stuff. It's pretty freaking irritating, but I'm not going to leave you. I mean, there are probably a lot of nasty things that I do, but you are still with me."

I thought for a moment. Then I said, "When I'm taking a bath and you barge in to go pee, it's pretty nasty. The toilet is less than a foot from the tub."

"That's it?" she asked.

"Well . . ." I started to say more, but she put her hand over my mouth.

"You know what; don't say anything more. I get it," she said.

She thought for a moment. Then she said, "None of that really matters. I still love you because you are a good dad and husband. I'm not all that I used to be." She gestured up and down with her hands. "I've got stretch marks and bags under my eyes. My arms flap like, like . . ." She struggled for a simile, "flags on a ship. I fart, too. But I don't think it's about that anymore. The sexiest thing you can do right now is be a good dad."

I gave her a confused look, so she went on, "It just seems to be about more, now. It's about dedication and working for our family." She mentioned how I go to work each morning. Then I come home, pitch in with the kids. How I bring her flowers and send her texts letting her know that I love her. "That's the sexy stuff. Not that I love how you snore or still leave the toilet seat up or fart in the van. That stuff's nasty. But the other stuff is more important."

"So what you are saying is, you aren't going to leave me because I snore?"

"No," she said. "But if you ever leave me because I pee while you take a bath, I'm posting this recording online and tagging you."

"That's cold," I said.

She winked.

> "SO WHAT YOU ARE SAYING IS, YOU AREN'T GOING TO LEAVE ME BECAUSE I SNORE?"... "NO" SHE SAID. "BUT IF YOU EVER LEAVE ME BECAUSE I PEE WHILE YOU TAKE A BATH, I'M POSTING THIS RECORDING ONLINE AND TAGGING YOU."

"How about you just delete that sucker right now?"

I reached for her phone, and she tugged it away. We playfully wrestled on the bed for a bit. Then we stopped. I held her close. We kissed. "I find you more attractive because you are a good mom. I hope you know that. I feel the same way about you."

We kissed again, and it felt like, for a moment, that this would lead to something more.

Then I felt someone watching us. Norah was

in the doorway. She asked for some cereal. I put my head into one of the pillows and said, "Just a minute."

I got up, and right before I left the room Mel said, "That. Right there. That's you being a cute dad."

I blew her a kiss and went to get Norah some breakfast.

SLEEP IS CURRENCY
IN MARRIAGE

Mel walked in on me sleeping. It was 2:00 p.m. on a Saturday, and I was supposed to be folding laundry.

"*Seriously?*" she said. "Why do you get a nap?"

"I'm not napping," I said. "I just fell over. Then I realized how comfortable the bed was, so I decided to stay in it for a little bit."

She didn't laugh.

"I want a nap," she said.

"Then take one," I said. My face was in the pillow, so I sounded muffled.

"*We* don't have time to nap." She emphasized the "we."

"Tristan has a soccer game in twenty minutes.

After that, Norah has a dance recital. After that, we have to go to the grocery store. We need to get the laundry done so it doesn't pile up . . ."

She went on listing all the things we needed to do this Saturday, and it felt like another workday. Ever since we had kids, every day has felt like a workday, even weekends and holidays. All I ever wanted to do was sleep.

EVER SINCE WE HAD KIDS, EVERY DAY HAS FELT LIKE A WORKDAY.

She finished with her list, then she stomped out of the room. I felt guilty. Not guilty enough to jump out of bed and apologize. I didn't feel that guilty. It was more of a "lie here and think about what I've done" guilty. I knew the right thing to do was to get up, but the guilt and how comfortable I felt in bed kept me down. That, and the fact that we'd each been up a couple of times that night. Getting all three of our children to sleep for more than five hours was about as likely as passing a bill into American law.

It happened, sometimes, but ultimately it took an act of God.

One child would be thirsty at 10:00 p.m., and by midnight another would be having a nightmare. The really difficult one was Aspen. She would stay up late fussing, and then would get up in the night at least once. I would drink an alarming amount of caffeine, and it got to the point that the bed, the sofa, the floor, really anything that I could lie down on, felt like a magnet.

GETTING ALL THREE OF OUR CHILDREN TO SLEEP FOR MORE THAN FIVE HOURS WAS ABOUT AS LIKELY AS PASSING A BILL INTO AMERICAN LAW.

There was another problem. Our days were hectic, too. I worked full-time plus, and Mel was a full-time mom and a part-time student. We had a house to care for, and something always seemed to be breaking or getting dirty. The older kids were in sports and Scouts, and a bunch of other wholesome activities that ate up the weekends. The previous Saturday, Tristan's soccer team had a doubleheader. Each game was in a different town, so I spent all day packing snacks for him and his team, driving him to pregame practice, the first game, to a warm-up and then to the second game. Once it was all said and done, this sweaty little boy in muddy cleats ate up the whole day. During the second game, I snuck into the van for a little shut-eye but then immediately felt guilty because it made me look like a parent sleeping at his son's soccer game, which I was. Yet I was so tired, I couldn't seem to help myself. I ended up sleeping for about ten minutes total, and on the drive home

Tristan said, "I can't believe you took a nap at my soccer game, Dad!"

Busted.

It was a total dick move . . .

I was exhausted *all* the time, and when it came to naps, I'd gotten pretty stealthy. I knew where to find a quiet, secluded sofa on my lunch break and how to fall asleep by leaning my head just right on the car window. But every once in a while, I'd get caught.

And then I'd feel guilty.

If you asked Mel what she wanted for her birthday, she'd say sleep.

SLEEP IS MORE IMPORTANT THAN PIZZA OR SEX.

I'd answer the same for all holidays. Scary Mommy once asked me to write a list of things husbands really want for Father's Day, and third on the list was sleep. It came below sex (number 1) and pizza (number 2). The list ended up being a topic of discussion on *The View*. The guest was Jim Gaffigan who placed sleep at the top of his list. Now, two years after writing the list, I agree with Jim.

Sleep is more important than pizza or sex.

As a parent with young kids, naps can really only happen when one parent watches all the kids while the other sleeps. Which essentially means that the parent who is awake is hanging out with the kids, doing the dishes or folding laundry, all the while bitterly thinking about the other sleeping comfortably in bed. It feels like an insult. Like a slap in the face. If one parent is sleeping, then the other parent is pissed off about it.

That is, unless there's a trade.

This is why sleep has become a black market item in our marriage. It can be traded for everything from manual labor to sex. It is the most powerful force in our marriage.

Two weekends before Mel caught me in bed when I was supposed to be doing laundry, I was in the yard pulling weeds. She approached me, reminded me about the long night she'd had with Aspen, and then said, "If you let me take a nap, we can have sex."

THIS IS WHY SLEEP HAS BECOME A BLACK MARKET ITEM IN OUR MARRIAGE. IT CAN BE TRADED FOR EVERYTHING FROM MANUAL LABOR TO SEX. IT IS THE MOST POWERFUL FORCE IN OUR MARRIAGE

She didn't wink. She didn't smile. She simply looked at me with the same straight-mouthed look I made when I put in my final offer on our house.

We negotiated for a little bit. I asked her if the sex would happen before or after the nap. We decided that it would have to happen after the kids went to bed that night. Then we shook hands and Mel went inside. I didn't feel bitter about her napping then. And I assume, in the past, when I'd offered her a child-free trip to Target or the day spa or some other thing she wanted in exchange for a nap, she didn't feel bad about letting me sleep. But it has gotten to the point that other than when one of us is sick, no one gets a nap unless there is a trade.

So when Mel caught me in bed without there having been any negotiation, she got angry. And, honestly, if the roles were switched, I'd have gotten angry, too. We've created this quid pro quo expectation when it comes to sleep, and me getting sleep for nothing was a lot like stealing.

I finally got up and walked into the kitchen. Mel was finishing the dishes.

MEL DID AN EPIC EYE ROLL, AND SOMEHOW I KNEW IF SHE HADN'T BEEN SO TIRED, SHE'D HAVE KILLED ME RIGHT THERE IN THE KITCHEN.

"I'm sorry. What do you want?" I said.

Mel was hunched over, starting the washer. She stood, looked at me and pushed up her glasses.

"How often do you do that?" she asked.

"Do what?"

"Sneak a nap?"

I shrugged.

I looked down.

Mel did an epic eye roll, and somehow I knew if she hadn't been so tired, she'd have killed me right there in the kitchen.

"Pump the brakes," I said. "Are you trying to tell me you never sneak a nap?"

Suddenly she was the one looking at the ground.

We were both guilty.

"Seriously, what do you want?" I said.

"What do you mean what do I want?" she said. "You know what I want. I want to take a nap. I want some sleep."

We went back and forth a bit, and as we did, I thought about parenting. Sometimes it feels thankless and exhausting. Sometimes it feels like I just want it all to slow down so I can sleep. And yet there is this part of me that understands that if it did actually slow down enough for me to sleep whenever I wanted, it would mean that it's over. It would mean that the children had moved out, and it would just be Mel and me living together. And the thought of that sounds pretty scary.

It feels like I missed it.

Mel and I eventually decided that she could take a nap while I took all three kids to Tristan's soccer game. When I got back, I could nap while Mel took the kids to the store. None of it was ideal.

Taking three kids to a soccer game was going to be hell. And I have to assume Mel felt the same way about taking all three kids to the store. But it would be worth it to take a nap.

By the end, we looked each other straight in the eyes, shook hands, and Mel said, "It's been nice doing business with you."

"Likewise," I said.

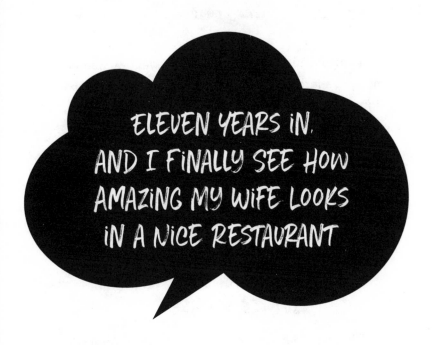

ELEVEN YEARS IN,
AND I FINALLY SEE HOW
AMAZING MY WIFE LOOKS
IN A NICE RESTAURANT

I was having dinner with Mel on a cruise ship. This was the first night of a seven-day cruise through the Caribbean, and each night we were scheduled to have dinner in the dining room, probably the nicest restaurant we'd ever been to. I was in a button-up shirt and slacks. Mel was in a nice off-white shirt with a brown skirt, her short brown hair curled. She looked beautiful, more so than I'd seen her look in a long time.

This is not to say that she didn't always look beautiful, because I always find her breathtaking, but there was something different about that dinner, and I think it was the setting. Behind her were windows looking out on the ocean. The sun was setting in orange and red and yellow. Behind me was a large crystal chandelier that cast just the right light, and below, on the first floor, musicians played acoustic versions of contemporary songs.

A FINE MEAL FOR US HAS ALWAYS BEEN SOMETHING LIKE THE OLIVE GARDEN. AND YOU KNOW WHAT? THE OG IS GREAT AND ALL, BUT IT REALLY IS THE IHOP OF ITALIAN RESTAURANTS. IT'S NOT BAD, BUT IT'S NOT GREAT.

This was our eleven-year anniversary. Over the years of college and kids and struggling to make ends meet, a fine meal for us has always been something like the Olive Garden. And you know what? The OG is great and all, but it really is the IHOP of Italian restaurants. It's not bad, but it's not great. No one is all that impressed by going there, and yet no one ever turns it down.

The year before I'd gotten a new, better-paying job, but even though we could afford more, we'd stuck with going to the same kinds of places. Or should I say, I'd stuck with the same places. I'm not the kind of person to get dressed up. I've worn a tuxedo three times in my life: at my sister's wedding, my brother's wedding and my own wedding. All three times sucked. In fact, I felt a little out of place when we first entered that restaurant on the ship. I like things simple, which can easily be translated to I like things cheap.

I'VE WORN A TUXEDO THREE TIMES IN MY LIFE: AT MY SISTER'S WEDDING, MY BROTHER'S WEDDING AND MY OWN WEDDING. ALL THREE TIMES SUCKED.

This isn't to say that I see myself as cheap, but as I struggle to find an adjective that describes me as someone who falls between being cheap, and the kind of guy that isn't cheap, I realize that I must be at the bottom of the cheap meter.

Okay.

I said it.

Are you happy now?

I was a cheap dude who loved my wife but simply couldn't let go of my concern for money, so I did some stupid things like never taking Mel out to a decent place for the first eleven years of our marriage. I don't know if this makes me a bad guy, but it definitely doesn't make me a great guy. It makes me a dude who needs to figure out his priorities.

Did I redeem myself there?

Probably not.

In my defense, after my father left I learned a lot about what it means to go without. My mother struggled, and I saw that. I can still remember her sitting at the dinner table surrounded by bills, her hands in her blond curls trying to figure out how she was going to pay for it all. And I remember thinking that I'd never do that to my wife or my family. And I think that's why I'd never taken Mel out somewhere nice. I mean really nice. A place like where we were eating on the cruise.

I DID SOME STUPID THINGS LIKE NEVER TAKING MEL OUT TO A DECENT PLACE FOR THE FIRST ELEVEN YEARS OF OUR MARRIAGE. I DON'T KNOW IF THIS MAKES ME A BAD GUY, BUT IT DEFINITELY DOESN'T MAKE ME A GREAT GUY. IT MAKES ME A DUDE WHO NEEDS TO FIGURE OUT HIS PRIORITIES.

This was the biggest vacation we'd ever been on (this includes our honeymoon, which was spent in a small cabin in central Utah). The cruise was a high point, and after we'd gotten our salads and ordered our meals, I leaned across the table, took Mel's hand and said, "I'm sorry."

Mel looked at me with a furrowed brow. We'd been talking about the ship and the next day's excursion to Haiti before we had ordered. Nothing to be sorry about.

"For what?" she said.

"For never taking you someplace like this before. I've never taken you out for a really nice meal, and now that I can see how amazing you look in this setting, I realize what I've been missing . . . what we've been missing."

Mel gave me a sly half grin. She pulled the right side of her hair behind her ear.

"Do I look nice here, too?" I asked.

Mel laughed and said, "Yes. You look cute."

I smiled.

NOR DID SHE SAY I WAS A CRAPPY HUSBAND FOR NEVER TALKING HER OUT FOR A FANCY MEAL, WHICH WAS OBVIOUSLY LONG OVERDUE.

It was quiet for a moment, and I kind of waited for Mel to jump on the opportunity to say, "I told you so," but she didn't.

Nor did she say I was a crappy husband for never talking her out for a fancy meal, which was obviously long overdue. She just shrugged and said, "I love you."

There was simplicity in her eyes. A soft look of understanding that only comes from sticking it out in a marriage for a number of years with a pretty cheap guy who didn't see himself as all that cheap.

One thing I can say about our relationship, however, is that we work as a team. We discuss the numbers and the budget together. There are no secrets (at least not that I'm aware of). She knows as well as I do where we stand financially.

And although I appreciated her compassion for our situation, what I realized by actually getting dressed up and going someplace nice is that it wasn't a waste of money. I feel like traveling back in time with that knowledge and smacking myself in the face for being such a cheap prick.

In that moment, being somewhere nice with my wife felt like an investment in her.

In me.

In us.

I'd never looked at it like that before. Sure, I'd heard people tell me something similar, but I hadn't listened. Nor had I ever taken the time to actually do it, so I hadn't realized how a nice restaurant, no kids, could look so good on my wife. I hadn't realized that her voice could go so well with the music or that her smile could match the sunset or that her blue eyes shine a little brighter next to a chandelier. I know this is all a bit mushy, but in that moment I felt a simple resurgence of love for my wife, and all it took was a change of setting.

We finished dinner and left. I don't know if this changed Mel's expectations of going out. I don't know if she expected more from me. In some ways, it might be good if it did change her expectations. She was still the same woman I'd been married to for eleven years. That hadn't changed. But what had changed was that as we walked around the ship looking out on the ocean, I couldn't get the way she looked in the restaurant out of my mind, and I couldn't help but want to see her like that again and again.

PREGNANCY
AND
CHILDBIRTH

ALL THE THINGS I NEVER SHOULD'VE SAID TO MY PREGNANT WIFE

I have said some stupid, embarrassing, dickhead things during Mel's pregnancies. All three of them. Every single one. I'm not proud of it. Not at all. But I think a lot of young fathers say some stupid things. None of the things I said were intended to be offensive, but therein lies the problem. I honestly wish someone would have said, "Shut your stupid face, Clint. You're sounding like a jerk right now." But it never happened, so I'm going to have a candid conversation with my former self. My hope is that some of you future fathers out there can read this sucker and learn from my mistakes. You're welcome.

'I HOPE YOUR BOOBS STAY THIS BIG.' Hold the phone, big guy. Clint! Do you realize what you just said? You told your wife that you are not satisfied with her normal breast size, and you'd love for that to change. Now she has to deal with the idea that even if she gets back to her prepregnancy body, it will not be good enough for you. Dick move, friend. Dick. Move.

'EVERY TIME I LOOK AT YOUR PREGNANT STOMACH, I FREAK OUT A LITTLE.' Right, I'm sure that you're scared. Mel being pregnant represents new responsibility. But here's the deal. She's probably just as scared, if not more scared, and to top it off, she has to look forward to changing hormones, a sour stomach and pushing an eight-pound baby through the vagina you love so dearly. You're not helping. Try being more supportive. Try getting a little more excited. Kids happen. Don't look to your wife for emotional support. She's got enough to worry about without you moping around and complaining about responsibility. You will be fine. Stop dreading the future and enjoy the moment.

'ALL THIS BABY STUFF IS MAKING ME REALLY EXHAUSTED. I'M GOING TO TAKE A NAP.' Listen, dude. I get it. Having a baby is exhausting on everyone. But are you growing a baby? Are you creating life? No. You are just driving the car to the hospital. Sure, you can take a nap. But I'd suggest offering one to your wife first. She's currently generating skin and bone and everything else in between. Cool?

"NOW I HAVE SOMEPLACE TO SET MY DRINK" (PLACES CAN OF COKE ON MEL'S STOMACH).

Oh . . . funny. You just turned your wife into furniture. Sure, she's growing your baby. As if that wasn't enough, now she gets to hold your drink. Come on, man, she means more to you than a side table . . . right? How about you treat her that way? That would be the gentlemanly thing to do.

"YOU CAN STAY AT WORK A LITTLE LONGER. MY MOTHER WORKED UNTIL THE DAY SHE HAD THE BABY."

Pump the brakes, there, big guy. Let's unpack what you just said. First, you tried to shame your wife into working longer. Then you compared her to your mother while also using an ultimatum. Now if she doesn't work longer, she isn't as good as your mother. I give you props for packing so much douchebaggery into one statement, but none of this was necessary. I get it. Money is tight. You are about to have a baby. But trying to shame the woman you love, the future mother of your child, into working longer by pulling the old, "my mother . . ." card is pretty assholetastic. Next time your wife says she wants to take time off, I'd suggest talking to her about how she's feeling. And leave your mother out of it.

"IT FEELS LIKE I'M MAKING LOVE TO A REFRIGERATOR." *Really?* You're not funny. Just don't talk for a while and hope she will have sex with you again once this is all over.

"I THINK I'M GAINING SYMPATHY WEIGHT" (WINK). Nope. You are just getting fat because you can't lay off the burritos. Don't try to blame your poor eating habits on the baby. Just own the fact that you might be stress-eating Mountain Dew and bacon. And while you are at it, don't mention weight around your pregnant wife. She's not getting fat, you idiot. She's making a baby. *Huge* difference.

"YOU ARE SO HORMONAL! IT'S DRIVING ME CRAZY." Good job stating the obvious, moron. Yes, pregnancy makes a woman crazy, weepy, ragey. You still have the power to regulate your emotions and hormones. Congratulations. You're not getting struck with sudden sorrow and frustration along with hot flashes and cravings for Taco Bell mild sauce. The closest thing you've had to a hot flash was the last time you ate at Buffalo Wild Wings. And it was a good flash, and the tears you shed were of joy. Stop making the assumption that if your wife is crying it's for no good reason and she needs to toughen up, or some other masculine crap. Just give her a hug. Ask how you can help. Let her have a moment alone. It's not that hard.

You knew this would happen. A million people

told you, and you saw it on a million TV shows. No surprises. But that doesn't invalidate her thoughts and feelings, or mean that something isn't important. Sure . . . you asked her to water the Christmas tree and she had a meltdown. That doesn't mean you need to act like she has a serious problem. The only problem she has is the baby you placed inside her. That's temporary. She is still the woman you love. You are in this together. Don't react with anger. React with compassion.

Okay, most of these statements were said innocently, right? But I suppose that's how it always starts with me. I say something without thinking, and then, bam! Foot in my mouth. And if I've learned anything from putting my foot in my mouth, it's this: Think twice, think three times before making a comment, and be quick to apologize.

GET THIS . . .
SEX IS A VERY SMALL PART
OF BABY MAKING

Mel was showing me one of her period-tracking calendars. She'd downloaded a few apps to help monitor her cycle: My Days, Period Tracker, Period Diary, etc. The one that caught my attention was Strawberry Pal. This app used strawberries to signify the days when she was on her period and bananas to show when she was the most fertile. She consulted these calendars all the time, showing me the banana days with a sly smile that seemed to say, *Buckle up, buddy*, and informing me about how accurate this calendar was at predicting her period.

Tristan and Norah were in the living room watching TV. Mel and I were in the dining room of our small apartment. Money was tight at the time, and I still couldn't believe that I'd agreed to have a third child. It was a religious thing, actually. I had prayed about it and felt strongly that we were supposed to have a third child. And having another child while pinching every penny was a huge leap of faith.

SEX SHOWED UP AS HEARTS, AND I RECALL LOOKING AT THE SPARSE HEARTS AND THINKING THAT EVEN WHILE TRYING TO HAVE A BABY, WE STILL HAD WHAT VISUALLY APPEARED TO BE A SAD AMOUNT OF SEX.

"It was exact," Mel said. "It knew the very day I was supposed to start my period." She spoke like Strawberry Pal was an intimate friend, a confidant she could tell anything she wanted to about her cycle and our sex life. It held all the calculations of her inner workings and displayed the results as emojis. Sex showed up as hearts, and I recall looking at the sparse hearts and thinking that even while trying to have a baby, we still had what visually appeared to be a sad amount of sex. Hearts scattered the calendar, one here and one there. Seeing it all laid out in front of me made me feel pathetic, particularly when I considered how spent I was.

In my teens I thought a lot about sex. I thought about how badly I wanted it.

Who am I kidding, I thought a lot about sex during this time, too.

I think a lot about sex now.

No surprises.

But sex changed after having kids. Not the actual act of sex, that stayed the same. In fact, at times, our moves got a little too consistent. Bada bing, bada boom. Yada yada yada. Hit the shower. I mean, it was all good. But I have to admit there was a certain consistent rhythm that started after having children that made sex feel a lot like when someone takes the same route to work each day.

As a teen I simply thought about sex. Period. It was something I desired and would do almost anything for. And I wrongly assumed that I'd always see it that simply. But as a father of two trying to make ends meet, combined with my understanding that parenthood is the most heartwarming, but also the most stressful and costly thing I'd ever done, having sex to make a baby felt weighty. Sometimes, it even felt like a chore, something I never in a million years thought I'd say.

To complicate it further, while trying to conceive our third child, we had what felt like an incredible amount of sex, despite what Strawberry Pal was showing me. I couldn't shake Mel off, and I felt more and more used. Sex happened whether I wanted it or not, and it was strange to be the one to say, "I've got a headache," or "Not tonight, I'm gassy," or "It's a little late, don't you think?" or some other cliché excuse for not being in the mood. It did, however, feel good to know that I could turn Mel down and she would come back around soon enough. And I suppose in those moments, when Mel was the sexual pursuer, I started to understand why she so often was willing to turn me down. She knew that I'd just keep wanting her, desiring her, knocking on her door.

Strawberry Pal also allowed Mel to use an emoji to show how she felt on a particular day. I'm not sure why her emotional state was important to conception, but what I do know is that one day showed two hearts and a smiley face.

"NO. I CAN'T RECALL WHY I WAS IN A GOOD MOOD THAT DAY, BUT I DOUBT IT HAD ANYTHING TO DO WITH SEX."

"What does the smiley mean?" I asked.

"It means I was in a good mood," she said.

"Was it because we had sex twice that day?"

She laughed like I was crazy.

"No. I can't recall why I was in a good mood that day, but I doubt it had anything to do with sex."

I scoffed and waved my hand in the air, clearly put out.

Mel rolled her eyes.

I did the same.

We looked at each other for a while without

speaking. It felt like we were going to get in a fight, which felt odd considering we'd fought in the past about sex. Only it never had anything to do with having too much sex or calculating sex or baby-making sex. It was usually because I was in the mood for sex and she wasn't.

"What's your problem?" Mel asked. She gestured at all the hearts on the computer screen. Then she leaned back in her chair, folded her arms and looked at me with a mix of confusion and frustration.

"Yeah," I said. "That's cool and all, but having sex for a baby feels . . ." I paused for a moment and searched for the right word, "confusing."

Every time we had sex, it was a reminder that we were going to have another baby. And I know, I get it, I agreed to have another child, and I wanted another child, but I was also really nervous about how we were going to afford another child, and that was making sex complicated.

Mel put her head back, opened her mouth and groaned into the air. This was something she often did when she couldn't, for the life of her, figure me out.

"I'm so lost right now," she said. "Am I doing something wrong? I thought you wanted another baby. How can we have another baby without sex?"

There was something about Mel coming at me with not exactly desire, but rather the white-hot heat of wanting a baby that made me feel like a piece of baby-making meat, and, to be honest, I realized that so much of this all came down to responsibility.

RATHER THAN EXPLAIN THIS ALL TO MEL IN SOME COHERENT WAY, I LET MY MIXED FEELINGS SQUEEZE MY THOUGHTS OUT SIDEWAYS.

At the time I was working full-time at the university and teaching close to full-time online. And yet we were still only scraping by. And despite all that, there we were, trying for a third. And when I think about that now, I realize that I was coming to terms with the true reality of sex. It meant children, which ultimately meant additional obligations and stress.

Rather than explain this all to Mel in some coherent way, I let my mixed feelings squeeze my thoughts out sideways.

"I'm not even excited about sex anymore," I said. "It just feels like work that's going to lead to more work."

Mel let out a breath and crossed her legs beneath the table. I couldn't tell if she was just frustrated by the fact that we were, for once, having more sex, but I still wasn't happy, or if she felt I was being confusing and frustrating and overthinking this whole thing. The sad part is, both were true, but I was too emotional to realize it.

"You know what," she said. "You just want sex to be about a good time, but it isn't anymore. It's about responsibility and love and . . . well, making babies. That doesn't mean you can't be excited and you can't enjoy it. You love the kids, right?" she asked.

Mel nodded her head and looked me in the eyes, hoping that I would begin nodding along with her.

I nodded, reluctantly.

"I've grown more in love with you because you've taken on the responsibility of being a father. Right now, to me as a mother, that's what makes you sexy."

In the moment, I didn't understand, so I got frustrated and left the table. I wouldn't say that I was angry; I just felt more confused than when we had begun the conversation.

It happened much faster than I expected. We didn't have any false alarms or several months of anticipation leading up to a letdown. We didn't have to visit any doctors to ask the difficult question: "Why can't we get pregnant?"

That all happened with our first child.

It took a little over a month of trying.

I got the news in Chicago. I was attending a conference for work. I was two hours ahead of Oregon, where Mel was, so I was asleep when she sent a photo to my phone of a little white stick that read *yes* in black letters.

There was no caption, but none was needed.

I stayed in bed for a while. My boss, David, was sleeping in the bed across from me. Most of the night he sounded like a whale, with his long gargling intakes of air and sloppy exhales. I was tired from traveling and the conference and the long, noisy nights. But once I saw the text, I regained some energy.

When Mel told me she was pregnant with Tristan, I sat down in the shower and cried. I was experiencing a mix of fear and anxiety. All of it was terrifying, and I didn't know how to cope with it. I don't think I've ever told anyone about that, not even Mel. When Mel told me she was pregnant the second time, I felt a similar feeling of fear and anxiety, only this time it was not as strong. Nevertheless, I still got real quiet and locked myself in the bedroom for a while. As I write, I'm starting to realize how emotional I've been.

With our third, though, I just looked at the phone. I wondered if I could handle the sleepless nights, poopy bums and messy sofas. I thought about how the kids will outnumber us. They were in control now.

And then I thought about responsibility. I thought about the fact that, once again, I was taking on more. And then I thought about what Mel said that day we argued in the kitchen. "I've grown more in love with you because you've taken on the responsibility of being a father. Right now, to me as a mother, that's what makes you sexy."

FOR SOME REASON I'D NEVER UNDERSTOOD THAT PART OF THIS TRANSITION WAS REALIZING THAT SEX, SEX APPEAL AND EVERYTHING TO DO WITH SEX AND ATTRACTION HAD BECOME ASSOCIATED WITH THE MOST UNSEXY THING I COULD THINK OF AS A YOUNG MAN: RESPONSIBILITY.

How I reacted in this moment would define who I was as a father. Taking this on, not freaking out, being strong about it, getting excited rather than being scared, was what a father did. And while I missed when sex seemed carefree, I was gaining something else with each step toward adulthood. It felt like I'd suddenly realized I was changing into some new thing, and it had been gradually happening for years, I just hadn't seen it. I was turning into a father. While I'd been telling people I was a father for years, for some reason I'd never understood that part of this transition was realizing that sex, sex appeal and everything to do with sex and attraction had become associated with the most unsexy thing I could think of as a young man: responsibility.

I'd never thought about it that way, but once I did, I knew that I didn't need to be so afraid. I needed to buy in.

I went to the lobby and called Mel. When she picked up I said, "Here we go again."

She laughed.

"Are you okay?" she asked.

"I think so."

I thought about the ebb and flow of my life. I thought about the joy mixed with frustration that children bring.

"Are you excited?"

I was quiet for a moment.

"Yes," I said. "I am."

"That's probably the sexiest thing you've ever said."

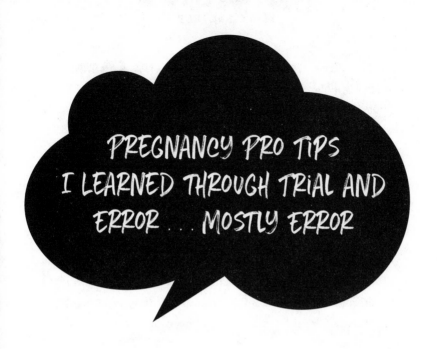

PREGNANCY PRO TIPS I LEARNED THROUGH TRIAL AND ERROR ... MOSTLY ERROR

When my wife was pregnant with our first child, Tristan, I received a lot of advice on how to best live with a pregnant woman. Most of it was warm and fuzzy. Some of it was meant to be helpful and show me how to be supportive. But none of it *really* showed the wonderful and crazy reality of living with someone expecting a baby.

In fact, a lot of it set me up for failure. So I think it's time to get real. I won't bullshit you. Let's bring it down a level. Here are the pregnancy pro tips I wish I'd been given:

TAKE NOTES WHEN YOU'RE SENT OUT FOR A CRAVING. COMING HOME WITH THE WRONG TACO SAUCE COULD GET YOU KILLED. I was once sent to Taco Bell at 10:00 p.m. for a Taco Supreme with specific instructions to bring home mild sauce. I forgot the sauce, which resulted in Mel crying because her real craving wasn't for the taco but for the sauce. This seemed crazy to me, and I foolishly argued with her about how foolish it was, causing the crying to turn into hysteria. I had to go back and get sauce, and once I got home, the tacos were cold, which resulted in a third trip. Long story short, it was after midnight before we got it all sorted out, and I almost spent the night on the sofa.

COMPARING A PREGNANT WOMAN TO LARGE OBJECTS (HOUSE, WHALE, REFRIGERATOR) MAKES YOU AN INCONSIDERATE DOUCHEBAG. I told Mel she was a "whale of a wife" while she was pregnant. Then I patted her tummy. I *did* sleep on the sofa that night. Wait . . . that's not accurate. I spent the night on the sofa. I didn't sleep.

THE SEXIEST THING AN EXPECTANT FATHER CAN DO IS ATTEND OB-GYN APPOINTMENTS. You know what's more boring than an ob-gyn appointment? Let me know once you have an answer for that question. Okay. Hold it. I take some of that statement back. It was really exciting the first time we heard the heartbeat. And the ultrasound is really cool. But other than that, it was boring. I'm sorry. But what I'm trying to get at is that having a baby isn't about entertainment. It's about life changes, and, most importantly, it's about supporting your pregnant wife. The least you can do is go to the doctor with her. That's the bar. When Mel had our second child, I didn't actually meet the doctor until the delivery, and when I think about that, it makes me a totally unsupportive jerk face. Hands down. Moral of the story? Don't be a jerk face like me.

WHEN A PREGNANT WOMAN CRIES, THE BEST THING TO DO IS NOT SPEAK. I learned the hard way to simply put my arm around Mel whenever she cried (see "whale of a wife" example).

HAND OVER ALL RIGHTS TO THE THERMOSTAT. IT'S EASIER THAT WAY. Mel once ended an argument over how cold she was keeping the house with, "You can take off clothing to cool down. I can't take out this baby!" That seemed to put things into perspective.

A MAN'S OLD SWEATPANTS AND T-SHIRTS ARE NOT A SATISFACTORY SUBSTITUTE FOR MATERNITY CLOTHING, SO KEEP THAT LITTLE BUDGET SAVER TO YOURSELF. I made this suggestion. I even laid out a few choice clothing options for Mel on our bed. I winked and told her how cute she would look in a man's flannel shirt and sweatpants. "It'll be like the '90s grunge scene!" I said.

"Is it that you want me to look like your twin

or some homeless pregnant woman you care for?" Then she locked herself in the bathroom. The next day we ordered a maternity wardrobe online.

COMPARING MORNING SICKNESS TO BEING HUNG OVER IS FUNNY FOR ABOUT THREE SECONDS. TRUST ME. The first time I made that comparison, Mel laughed. The second time, she smiled. The third and fourth . . . well . . . you get the idea.

WHEN SENT OUT FOR PASTRIES OR OTHER BAKED GOODS, SEND CELL PHONE PHOTOS OF ALL AVAILABLE PASTRIES AND BAKED GOODS. THIS WILL SAVE YOU A SECOND TRIP TO THE STORE. Send pictures, send pictures, send pictures (shaking my head with regret).

PREGNANCY TENDS TO TURN UP THE VOLUME ON EVERYTHING. ESPECIALLY HOW MUCH A HUSBAND SNORES. DON'T TAKE IT PERSONALLY WHEN YOU'RE SLEEPING IN ANOTHER ROOM. I actually had a hard time with this one. It felt like I was being sent away for something I couldn't control. It only happened around the end of the pregnancy, and once the baby was born, I was back in our old bed, snoring away.

NEVER USE THE WORD 'CANKLE.' Mel and I have a pretty sarcastic relationship, and I thought we could handle something like this. I was wrong. Very wrong. Mel was already self-conscious about her pregnant body, and saying something stupid like "cankle" when she started to retain water and couldn't fit into her shoes made me an inconsiderate dick.

NEVER QUESTION HOW OFTEN A PREGNANT WOMAN NEEDS TO PEE. JUST ASSUME THAT SHE ALWAYS NEEDS TO PEE. NEEDING TO PEE IS A PREGNANT WOMAN'S DEFAULT. And don't comment on it, roll your eyes, moan or tell stupid jokes at dinner parties about how many times you stopped while taking a drive across the country. Just let her pee in peace.

NINETY PERCENT OF BEING WITH A PREGNANT WOMAN IS REASSURING HER THAT SHE WILL BE A GREAT MOTHER. There was a reason Mel was dog-earing and underlining her copy of *What to Expect When You're Expecting*. She wanted to know what was going to happen, surely, but she was also searching for reassurance. I didn't figure that out until after we had our first child. What Mel really wanted to hear from me was, "You're going to be a great mother."

COMPARING A CHILD KICKING INSIDE THE WOMB TO A SCENE FROM THE SCI-FI FILM *ALIEN* IS BASICALLY TELLING A PREGNANT WOMAN THAT SHE'S CARRYING AN ALIEN. You do the math.

DON'T BE AFRAID TO ARGUE WITH A PREGNANT WOMAN ABOUT HOW BEAUTIFUL SHE IS. Mel had a nasty habit of telling me how ugly she was while pregnant. She commented on her skin, which was getting red and blotchy. She commented on how big she was getting and how she couldn't see her feet anymore. I argued with her every time, reminding her how beautiful she was. How amazing and dedicated she was to put her body through all this. I think I got that part right.

SPOIL HER. SHE'S GROWING YOUR CHILD. Enough said.

Sure, there are more tips. There always are. But this should get expectant fathers started. And if you are reading this list to a new father in your life, add a few specific tips. New fathers can use all the help they can get—trust me.

MATERNITY LEAVE ISN'T A VACATION

We were in the driveway of the two-bedroom 1950s farmhouse we were renting in Provo, Utah. This must have been 2007. Mel'd just gotten off work at her hardware store job. We were about to go grocery shopping. She was incredibly pregnant. Just-about-to-pop pregnant. Her due date was over a month away; however, she'd be having the baby in a couple of days. Obviously I didn't know this at the time. I didn't realize that Mel had preeclampsia and that she'd need an emergency C-section.

Neither of us did.

In the back seat, ready to rock, was a car seat for our first child. Mel tried to reach down and rub her ankles, but her pregnant belly got in the way.

"I can't wait to get this kid out," she said. "I'm so tired." She put her head back and closed her eyes, and I said, "At least you get a vacation. You are going to have four weeks off."

I raised my eyebrows and looked at her. My face seemed to say, "Lucky."

SHE DIDN'T SAY ANYTHING, AND LIKE AN IDIOT, I ASSUMED THIS WAS HER WAY OF SAYING THAT SHE AGREED WITH ME. SHE'S EASING INTO THE SEAT, I THOUGHT. SHE'S LOOKING FORWARD TO SOME TIME OFF AFTER HAVING A BABY. I WAS WRONG … REALLY WRONG.

She opened her eyes and gazed at the tan car ceiling. Looking back on this moment, I know she was irritated. Four-alarm, you-said-something-really-stupid irritated. But the sad fact is I wasn't so good with nonverbal cues or hints or language that directly told me that Mel was one click away from burying me in a cold, cold grave.

She was nine months pregnant and still going into work, her stomach far out into space, her small frame chugging on, her torso off-kilter like a muffin on its side, trying to sell gardening tools and plants at a hardware store. I often went home from work because of a sniffle, while Mel chugged along, working 40 hours a week while growing a baby in her body, her ankles smooth as sausages.

She didn't say anything, and like an idiot, I assumed this was her way of saying that she agreed with me. *She's easing into the seat*, I thought, *She's looking forward to some time off after having a baby*.

I was wrong.

Really wrong.

"How is this a vacation?" she asked.

"You aren't working," I said. "Sounds like vacation to me."

Mel didn't come back with a smart retort. She didn't tell me that one month off was not nearly enough time for her to fully recover physically from having a child, let alone gain a connection with our new baby. She didn't talk about how the big-box, multibillion dollar a year hardware store she worked for only provided four weeks of maternity leave, which was really frustrating and unethical. She didn't talk about how she wouldn't be able to take any time off before having the baby, even though she was tired and swollen and pregnant, and more or less slogged through her shifts each day on her feet the whole time, forcing herself to endure it all because she was afraid that if she used any time off before having the baby, she wouldn't have enough time left after having the baby to recover.

Instead, it all came out in a big boogery mess

that drained down her poor sad swollen face. She looked at me like I was the most inconsiderate dickhead in the history of dickheads. With violent jerking arm movements, she struggled to unbuckle herself from the slightly used Mazda Protegé we had purchased a few weeks earlier. I tried to help her with the buckle, and she slapped my hand as if it was something nasty, so I pulled away. Once she was free from the belt, she struggled to open the car door. Then she worked her small, heavily weighted frame out of the car and waddled into the house, slamming the side screen door, and then slamming the wooden side door for good measure.

I WENT AHEAD AND ASSUMED SHE LOCKED HERSELF IN THE BEDROOM. I WAS RIGHT ABOUT THAT. I WAS ALSO RIGHT TO ASSUME THAT I'D BE SLEEPING ON THE SOFA.

A moment later I heard her slam another door inside.

I went ahead and assumed she locked herself in the bedroom. I was right about that. I was also right to assume that I'd be sleeping on the sofa. I bring this up because I wasn't right about a lot of things in this moment, so it feels good to let you all know that I wasn't a complete idiot.

I sat in the car for some time looking at the

open field behind our house, trying to figure out what I had done wrong. Part of me assumed that she was just being hormonal. I did that a lot during the first pregnancy. This is a problem that many men run into. I thought that Mel was acting irrationally because she was pregnant. But the reality was, regardless of her hormones, she was pissed off at me because I was being insensitive. Sure, she was probably more emotional than she might have been if she wasn't pregnant, but that doesn't change the fact that I wasn't really looking at the full situation.

We were broke. We lived paycheck to paycheck. I was waiting tables and attending college, and Mel was working full-time at the hardware store. Between both of our paychecks and student loans, we barely made ends meet without a child. I had no idea how we were going to support a baby, and yet we were having one. Mel and I did the budget together. She was well aware that without her paycheck each week, we'd never make it. No way. Although I didn't realize it at the time, she must have felt a lot of pressure to get back to work and help support our family. Then, in addition, she also had the fears all first mothers have about the birthing process. And despite all this, I was calling her maternity leave a vacation in a way that made it sound like I was jealous.

I went in the house and knocked on the bedroom door. She didn't answer. I called her cell.

Nothing.

I spent that night on the sofa, not sleeping, trying to understand why I was in trouble but not wanting to bring up the subject again. This happened a lot early in our marriage. I wasn't sure what I had done wrong, but I didn't want to push it and cause another argument, so I just didn't mention it again. It took me a few more years to realize that the best thing to do, at least for us, was to let it settle for a day, then ask what happened and try to find a resolution.

Because Mel had a cesarean, rather than a vaginal birth, she was granted two extra weeks of maternity leave.

Throughout those six weeks, I didn't question my assumption that maternity leave was a vacation. I didn't question it as I helped Mel get out of bed so she wouldn't tear her stitches. I didn't question it as she bled for days after the procedure, all the while trying to get our son to figure out how to latch on properly to nurse. I didn't question it during all the times I had to leave for work or class, worrying the whole drive about Mel at the house, alone with our new baby and her healing body. And I didn't question it when Mel cried because she had to quit breastfeeding because her job didn't provide her a secluded space to pump outside of their public restroom.

It wasn't until we dropped off our six-week-old son at Mel's mother's house so Mel could return to work that I finally questioned my assumption.

My mother-in-law agreed to watch our son for free while I attended classes and Mel worked.

Mel stood in her parents' driveway and cried. I tried to console her, but it didn't help. She cried. And as she cried, she flinched with each intake of air and held her abdomen.

This was nothing hormonal. This had nothing to do with carrying a baby, because that time had passed. It had nothing to do with the drudgery of going back to work after taking some time off.

It had to do with the fact that Mel was not physically or emotionally healed enough to go back to work, and yet she had to.

It wasn't until I added it all up that I realized maternity leave was far from a vacation. It wasn't even close.

Mel finally calmed down, and we both stood in my in-laws' driveway next to our parked cars. She was in brown corduroy maternity pants and a loose blue maternity shirt, her body still a little swollen.

IT WASN'T UNTIL I ADDED IT ALL UP THAT I REALIZED MATERNITY LEAVE WAS FAR FROM A VACATION. IT WASN'T EVEN CLOSE.

I wouldn't see her until around midnight, after my shift waiting tables.

I gave her a hug, and I told her that I was sorry.

She looked up at me and said, "It's okay. It will all be okay. Mom will take good care of Tristan, and work will be over soon."

"Yeah," I said. "That's true. But that's not what I'm saying. I'm sorry for calling your maternity leave a vacation. It wasn't even close."

Mel thought for a moment. Her blue eyes went from side to side. She'd obviously forgotten about the argument.

"I didn't realize how difficult all this would be. I'm sorry."

She didn't say anything. She just put her face in my chest. And as she did, I felt like a failure. I felt like I wanted to give her more. I was angry with myself for waiting to go to college. I was angry that our situation wasn't better. And as I watched her drive away, I thought about how strong Mel was. I thought about how I hoped that after college things would get better for us.

Our situation did, in fact, improve. With our next two children, Mel was able to take off as much time as she needed. And with each child after Tristan, I never used the word *vacation* when describing her maternity leave. Instead, I used the word *recovery*.

I also never slept on the sofa again.

Okay, I'm sorry. That was a lie.

I WASN'T MAN ENOUGH TO WITNESS CHILDBIRTH

It was late afternoon when Mel called.

"The doctor said we are having the baby today. How soon can you be to the hospital?"

I didn't know what to say outside of "Really?" I kept repeating it until Mel told me to be quiet. Then she told me she had preeclampsia and the doctor was going to perform an emergency C-section. I was 24, and Tristan was coming two weeks early because Mel's feet, hands, face—all of her—swelled up. I didn't know what preeclampsia was, I didn't realize it could be fatal if unchecked, and I *certainly* didn't realize that it could cause doctors to cut into my wife's stomach and take the baby out.

In fact, I didn't know that was even an option. It's almost laughable how little I knew about childbirth at the time. I was the youngest in my family. I learned about childbirth in high school biology, but it was a pretty surface-level education. No one told me that traditional birth included skin tearing, intense pain and involuntary pooping.

IT'S ALMOST LAUGHABLE HOW LITTLE I KNEW ABOUT CHILDBIRTH AT THE TIME.

Mel talked me down like a suicide prevention officer in an '80s movie. She was the one having a baby, and yet I was the one freaking out. "I need you here," she said. "Please drive safe."

I went into the delivery room wrapped innocently in a white medical suit, mask, hat and booties.

Mel was sprawled out on a table, her shoulders and head sticking out from a curtain (behind which, I will admit, I was nervous to look). I didn't really know what to expect so I looked down, I looked at Mel, I looked *anywhere* but at the business end of my son's birth.

About twenty minutes in, I heard a baby cry, and the doctor said, "Daddy. Come see your son."

I assumed they were done.

I was wrong.

Before my wife's cesarean, I'd seen some really grotesque films. Movies showing people ripped apart or shot up or blown to bits. I'd seen almost every Schwarzenegger action film, even *Commando* where that no-name guy takes a saw blade to the head. I watched them all with my buddies while snacking on candy and chips and drinking cans of Coke. None of it fazed me. But nothing prepared me for my wife's cesarean.

Nothing.

MEL TALKED ME DOWN LIKE A SUICIDE PREVENTION OFFICER IN AN '80S MOVIE. SHE WAS THE ONE HAVING A BABY, AND YET I WAS THE ONE FREAKING OUT.

Reaching from a gaping hole in my beautiful wife's stomach was the head and right arm of a bloody, powder white, childlike creature. Something white and veiny was wrapped around his neck and shoulder that seemed unnatural, but thinking back it must have been the umbilical cord.

It felt like he was reaching out for me, and I couldn't tell if he wanted an embrace or to drag me down to hell.

I'd never had a major surgery myself, and I still haven't. The closest was my vasectomy, which happened years later and wasn't really major at all. I'd often heard people talk about the miracle of birth, which sounded very pleasant, but the actual *act* of a birth, the moment of, was hands down the most frightening thing I'd ever seen.

My knees went weak.

I felt queasy.

I sat down.

In fact, just writing about this is making me queasy again. Perhaps it's because I have a weak stomach. Maybe I simply can't handle that much blood and guts in real life. But honestly, I think it's because I'm simply not man enough to handle childbirth on any level.

PERHAPS IT WAS THE EPIDURAL, BUT MEL LOOKED AS CALM AS A HINDU COW. I WAS SITTING IN A CHAIR, A PALE WRECK OF A MAN . . .

I sat down and tried not to puke.

Mel looked up at me and said, "You look white. Are you okay?"

"Are *you* okay?" I asked. "You *don't* want to know what they're doing to you."

Perhaps it was the epidural, but Mel looked as calm as a Hindu cow. I was sitting in a chair, a pale wreck of a man, as Mel lay on the surgical table, doctors cutting her open, doing their business in what appeared to be the most terrifying actions I'd ever seen performed on another person. She smiled at me. Then she laughed. Not an evil laugh or a you're-pathetic laugh. It was more of a you're-cute laugh. It was the kind of laughing a man makes while at a haunted house with his girlfriend.

Once it was all said and done—once I was holding our son and Mel was stitched and bandaged and all our family had left—I can remember looking at Mel propped up in her hospital bed and realizing that if the roles had been reversed, I'd have cried like a girl. Which is funny to say, considering Mel is a woman, and she didn't cry, so perhaps I should say I'd have cried like a man, because I was clearly not strong enough to birth a child.

Up until we had children, I never thought of Mel as the strong one. I'm not sure if I saw myself as strong, either, but I felt that my job was to be strong. Not that I'm a particularly large or masculine person. I stand five foot seven. The joke around my hometown was that I actually lived in a tree and made fudge. But there was something about getting married and calling myself the man of the house that made me feel like I needed to be the strong one. I needed to be the one who got up in the night and searched the house when we heard a noise. I was the one who told Mel's former boyfriend to back off, or I'd kick his trash. Not that I'd done much trash kicking in my life, but I tried to sound convincing. I was the strong one with all the spiders.

I'd fallen into this tough-guy mind-set, all the while not realizing that Mel was actually the badass.

What shocked me the most was the next day when Mel was up walking around. Her steps were slow and soft. She held my hand to keep steady, but she was up. She was smiling.

I think a lot of people assume that the bravery of a mother is just something that mothers are supposed to do because it's been happening for so long. But, honestly, there is something inside a mother, some spark from God or genetics that makes them bring a baby into this world regardless of the pain and torment of their own body. Then she does everything possible to make sure her baby turns out healthy, happy and intelligent. And it all begins in a screaming bloody mess that, trust me, is terrifying to watch.

AND EVEN iF I DO GET A SCAR THAT EQUALS HERS, iT WiLL NEVER SiGNiFY NEARLY AS MUCH iMPORTANCE, BECAUSE iT WiLL HAVE TO DO WiTH MY SURVIVAL ALONE AND NOT THE CREATION OF LiFE.

Each one of our children has come via cesarean. And while I know there's a lot of discussion about the overuse of cesarean sections, that's not why I'm writing this essay. I'm writing it because across Mel's abdomen is a lengthy scar. It's deep and pink. It's larger than any scar I have or probably ever *will* have. And even if I do get a scar that equals hers, it will never signify nearly as much importance, because it will have to do with my survival alone and not the creation of life.

Her scar is evidence of dedication and determination to our family. It's evidence of her willingness to do whatever it took to bring our children into the world—a boy and two girls who fill my life with more joy than I ever thought possible. Every time I see it, I am filled with a swell of admiration for the mother of my children. And I'm reminded that I'm not woman enough to have a baby.

With her third and final cesarean, I recall Mel lying naked in front of a handful of doctors and nurses. Blood dripped from the sides of her hips; her stomach looked like a deflated balloon. All her coverings had been removed so she could be transferred from the surgical table to a rolling bed. I stood away from her, holding our new daughter, Aspen, who was sleeping soundly.

Mel joked with the doctor, casually chatting as though the two were at dinner. She was naked and cut and drugged, and yet she was happy and full of life. I was still a bit squeamish, but I couldn't help but notice how beautiful she looked with all that strength and dedication.

Mel looked up at me. She smiled. Not a forced smile, but a real one.

I smiled back and then held up our new daughter so she could take a look at what all her strength had accomplished.

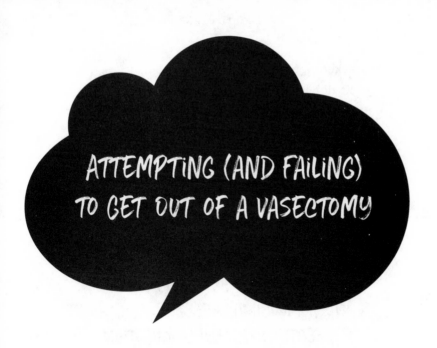

ATTEMPTiNG (AND FAiLiNG) TO GET OUT OF A VASECTOMY

I was sprawled out on a surgical table with no pants. In the room were two nurses and one short, chipper doctor. One nurse was blond, in her late 40s; the other was Hispanic and in her mid-30s.

Never before had so many people been staring at my genitals at the same time.

I couldn't feel pain, only pressure. I felt a pinch when the doctor gave me a couple of shots, and a little burning as he injected something into me. Before the surgery, I had been given a Valium. I asked to be sedated, instead they gave me a Valium. The doctor also asked if I wanted to watch, "We can move these so you can see," he said while pointing at some mirrors mounted above me.

I asked again if I could be sedated.

"We don't do that," he said. Then he offered me another Valium.

I accepted.

He asked me about my kids, and although this seemed like a perfectly reasonable question, considering I was getting a vasectomy, there was something ironic about it. Is that the word I want? *Irony*? Maybe not. Perhaps it's *finality*.

> ## HE ASKED ME ABOUT MY KIDS, AND ALTHOUGH THIS SEEMED LIKE A PERFECTLY REASONABLE QUESTION, CONSIDERING I WAS GETTING A VASECTOMY, THERE WAS SOMETHING IRONIC ABOUT IT.

The surgery was supposed to be performed by Doctor Hatchet. I met with her originally, and although she seemed pleasant enough, her name was terrifying. Combining how anxious I was about getting a vasectomy with having a female doctor named Hatchet performing the operation, I couldn't help but feel that I was the subject of a deep, dark joke perpetrated by God. I remember thinking, "Sure. Use a hatchet. I don't see how it could make getting a vasectomy any worse."

My schedule didn't work with Doctor Hatchet's, so I ended up with Doctor Fishburn, who was in his late 50s. He was short with graying black hair. He wore glasses, a red sweater vest, a white shirt and a black tie. He smiled most of the time, and at first I couldn't tell if he was just trying to keep things cool and casual or if it was his disposition.

COMBINING HOW ANXIOUS I WAS ABOUT GETTING A VASECTOMY WITH HAVING A FEMALE DOCTOR NAMED HATCHET PERFORMING THE OPERATION, I COULDN'T HELP BUT FEEL THAT I WAS THE SUBJECT OF A DEEP, DARK JOKE PERPETRATED BY GOD.

"I have three kids," I said.

I felt some pressure. I felt something being cut.

"Oh . . . that's wonderful," he said. He paused, leaned in closer to my crotch and looked at something. Then he stood upright, his hands working with the same casual rhythm one might use while making a spaghetti dinner.

As he worked, he told me about how he got a vasectomy while in the military. "I tried to run the next day. I ended up with pain in my testicles for the next 25 years. I tell every patient this story so they will take it easy. Healing is important."

I'd heard this from a few people. I'd heard a mix of stories about getting a vasectomy. I'd heard people tell me about being shaved by a large black man with cold calloused hands and a firm grip. I'd heard stories of people who had to have the vasectomy done twice because it didn't work the first time. One friend told me about how he couldn't take a bump on his bike for a few years because he'd be hit with a biting pain. It seemed like most men had a vasectomy horror story, and if they didn't, it was because they'd refused to get one. Then they'd tell me one of their friend's horror stories about getting a vasectomy.

This is part of the reason I initially refused to get a vasectomy.

Mel and I had talked about it a million times during our marriage. I'd always said that I was open to getting a vasectomy. After our third, however, as it became more and more obvious that we weren't going to have more children, I started getting cold feet. I kept putting off making the appointment despite Mel's weekly, sometimes daily, reminders.

"When are you going to make an appointment?"

"When are you going to make an appointment?"

"When are you going to make an appointment?"

Times infinity . . .

I relented, eventually, and that's when they sent me something I wish they hadn't.

A pamphlet.

Two weeks before the procedure I was in an easy chair reading *The Decision to Get A Vasectomy*. I think that's what it was called. It might have been,

What to Expect From Your Vasectomy, or maybe, *The Joy of the Vasectomy*. I can't recall the exact title. I simply recall that it felt stiff, like it was trying very hard to make men feel like they had some control over the situation and put them at ease about the whole ordeal.

It wasn't working.

Mel was in the dining room wearing jeans and an old gray-and-white-striped American Eagle shirt and working on a laptop. Parts of the pamphlet I read out loud to her, along with snippets of commentary. "Your testicles and scrotum are cleaned with an antiseptic and possibly shaved."

"That doesn't sound so bad . . ." I said.

"You may be given . . . medicine to reduce anxiety . . ."

"I like that kind of medication."

"Your doctor makes one or two small openings in your scrotum."

I let out a breath.

Then I read the list of signs that you might have an infection.

"Redness, swelling, fever or chills, fluid draining from . . ."

I stopped there.

I looked at Mel. She was looking down. I could tell that she was paying attention.

The whole idea felt so permanent and emasculating. And the funny thing is that Mel and I always agreed that I would be the one to get fixed, not her. Mainly because it is such a simple surgery for men, whereas for a woman, the procedure seems more complicated. Although, I must admit that we considered having her tubes tied when she gave birth to Aspen. We'd heard it's easier if done during a C-section. But we just didn't know if we were ready yet, so we waited.

I DON'T KNOW WHAT IT IS WITH MEN AND THEIR PENISES. I'M CONFUSED BY IT, TOO.

According to the pamphlet, my potential complications ranged from swelling and minor infection to not being sterilized. That last bit sounded kind of awesome, actually. It felt like I was too manly for modern doctors to handle. On the grand scale of complications, everything listed was minor. Yet I still had my anxieties, and I think so much of it came down to a deeper psychological fear of losing my masculinity. I don't know what it is with men and their penises. I'm confused by it, too. But what I do know is that from the beginning, the penis has been a huge topic of conversation. It started on the playground, and the conversation continued into scout camps and college locker rooms. A pit in my gut that I didn't fully understand, and didn't know if I ever would, formed at the thought of shooting blanks, and that was a huge part of my anxiety.

I didn't know just how to explain all of this to Mel, so instead I simply said, "I can't go through with this. I just can't. I'm sorry."

Mel rested her forehead on the table next to the laptop. "Does it really sound worse than what I've gone through?"

I don't think she meant this as a guilt trip, although it could easily be perceived that way. I think she said it out of something deeper. It came from someone whose body had taken years of pills to prevent pregnancy, then had stopped those pills so it could be opened up to pregnancy. It had grown our three children, been cut open three times and sewn back up three times. Her body had bled and produced milk. It carried scars and stretch marks. I can only imagine that the thought of something, anything, more sounded unbearable.

I DON'T THINK SHE MEANT THIS AS A GUILT TRIP, ALTHOUGH IT COULD EASILY BE PERCEIVED THAT WAY.

Mel reminded me of how during the birth of our last child, air got caught in her shoulders because of the cesarean and caused so much pain that she cried all night for two nights in the hospital. And as she spoke, I thought about how I was in the room for all three of our children's births but only watched the first one for about 30 seconds.

Childbirth was simply too real. Too gruesome. The day after each one, I'd watch Mel struggle to get up and walk around, and I realized that she's the strongest person I know. And when I thought about that, I considered that perhaps my priorities were not in the right place.

"I'm just really nervous," I said. "I hope it's okay for me to admit that."

Mel walked over and sat next to me on the sofa. "Yes," she said. "Absolutely."

Mel snuggled next to me, and suddenly she was giving me comfort. Which seemed strange. She'd been through so much to bring our children into the world, and yet there she was comforting me. But that really is the most remarkable part about Mel. She has empathy for everyone, and regardless of her own struggles and pain, she is able to put all of it aside and comfort the ones she loves most. All mothers are like this.

SAYING THAT I NEEDED TO MAN UP FOR MY VASECTOMY SEEMED SO STRANGE, BUT AT THE TIME IT MADE SENSE.

Eventually she went back to working on her laptop. We didn't talk about the vasectomy for a couple of days. I never canceled the vasectomy appointment, but I wanted to.

One morning as I was heading out to work, I

stopped Mel in the kitchen and said, "Don't worry about it. I'm nervous, but I'll get it done."

I didn't have to tell her what "it" was. She knew. I could see her body, her face, everything, go slack with relief.

"I'm sorry for saying I wouldn't. I'm just nervous, but I need to man up."

Saying that I needed to man up for my vasectomy seemed so strange, but at the time it made sense. Mel kissed me and said, "Thank you." And a few days later, I was sprawled out in the hospital with no pants on.

I WAS, FOR THE MOST PART, COMFORTABLE. WELL ... AT LEAST AS COMFORTABLE AS I COULD BE WITHOUT WEARING PANTS AND ON VALIUM.

As Doctor Fishburn worked on my body, we chatted about our kids. We shared a few stories. I was, for the most part, comfortable. Well . . . at least as comfortable as I could be without wearing pants and on Valium.

When I say it that way, it sounds very comfortable.

We told a few jokes. I told him about my blog. I told him that I'd appreciate it if he told everyone that I was so full of testosterone that I couldn't be sterilized.

I think that was the Valium talking.

And once it was all said and done and I had my pants back on and everyone was gone but the older nurse, who was reading a list of things I should know about aftercare, I suddenly became nauseous. I felt hot and tired and I had to lie down with a cool, wet towel on my head.

The nurse told me this was normal. "Lots of men have this problem." It almost felt as if she were trying to confirm that I was, in fact, still a man. And I got the impression that she'd been helping with vasectomies for a number of years.

"Do you have children?" I asked.

"Yes," she said. "But they are much older than yours. My youngest is fifteen."

She gave me a soft maternal smile and said, "My husband went through this, too. He survived. I'm sure you will, too."

"None of that really matters," I said. "I know I will survive. My wife birthed the kids. I saw it happen. It was horrible. This is the least I could do."

I thought about that a lot as the doctor was working on me. I thought about watching three children being cut from my wife. I thought about the large incision below her navel. I tried to think about that rather than the horror stories about vasectomies. I tried to think about that rather than the pressure. Or the nausea. Or the fact that although I was still a man, I was a man without seed. There was something about focusing on

Mel's strength that made it all bearable.

The nurse smiled at me and nodded. Then I started gagging. I leaned onto my side, but I didn't throw up.

The nurse rubbed my back.

I was sweating.

Then I lay back down, and she told me Mel was picking up my prescriptions and I needed to stay down until she arrived.

"You seem like a good guy," she said.

"Thanks," I said. "I needed to hear that right now."

PARENTING

I THOUGHT I WAS
A GOOD FATHER UNTIL I TOOK
MY TODDLER SHOPPING

I was grocery shopping with Aspen when she yanked a bottle of spaghetti sauce from the store shelf and threw it to the ground. Then she looked at me, emotionless, eyes steady, lips straight, as though she'd just dropped a mic. The sauce was everywhere: the cart, my pants and shoes, all the other bottles of sauce on the bottom shelf. This was after she'd thrown a handful of fits in the produce section because I wouldn't let her take a bite out of some dragon fruit or hold a watermelon.

Taking her to the store alone each week was a new thing. She was two, close to three. Mel was starting a garden at our children's school. She spent most Saturdays there, along with Tristan and Norah. So each Saturday, it was the toddler and me cleaning house and running errands while Mel went to work. The thing about Aspen was, she was basically a wild animal.

She was adorable, no doubt about it. She had blond hair that we often pulled into little pigtails. And her voice was somewhere between Peppa Pig and a songbird. Her smile was sweet but mischievous.

THE THING ABOUT ASPEN WAS, SHE WAS BASICALLY A WILD ANIMAL.

Ultimately, though, she didn't care.

She was the child running to the pulpit at church each Sunday with Dad chasing her, hoping to catch her right before she could slam her little hands down on the organ keys. She was the child ripping at the artificial plants at the doctor's office or sneaking away to pound the computer keys and mess up some poor patient's file. She was the child who, regardless of how far I parked the cart away from the grocery store shelf, still managed to grab a bottle of spaghetti sauce and smash it to the ground, covering my legs and one shoe with Newman's Own Sockarooni.

The really difficult part was her innocence. I couldn't really blame her for anything, although I wanted to. So I just ended up feeling like a failure as a parent, like I'd done something wrong because she acted like a nut job, when, in fact, the real problem was her age.

Sometimes she threw fits; other times she moved like a ninja from one problem to the next. I'd take a pen away from her, and as I'd place it back in the desk drawer, she'd pick up a doll stroller and attempt to smash the TV screen.

> AND WHEN I THINK ABOUT THAT, IT FEELS LIKE GOD OR SOME OTHER HIGHER POWER PULLED A BAIT AND SWITCH OF SOME KIND, GIVING US TWO RELATIVELY EASY TODDLERS IN COMPARISON TO ASPEN, WHO WAS LIKE LIVING WITH A RABID RACCOON ON A POT OF COFFEE.

This isn't to say that she was abnormal. She was two. They call it the terrible twos for a reason. But that doesn't mean I was any less embarrassed as a parent when my toddler broke stuff. It was embarrassing, flat-out 100 percent, and I will be the first to admit that I wasn't thrilled to be taking her to the store each week. Not that I hadn't taken a toddler to the store. Obviously I had. She was my third. But the joke in our house was that if Aspen had been our first, she'd have been our last. And when I think about that, it feels like God or some other higher power pulled a bait and switch of some kind, giving us two relatively easy toddlers in comparison to Aspen, who was like living with a rabid raccoon on a pot of coffee.

The embarrassing part about it all, even more embarrassing than the spaghetti sauce incident, was how cocky I'd been about spending Saturdays alone with her. Naturally this was a change in our lives. Mel only started working at Tristan and Norah's school a few months earlier. Before that first Saturday, Mel gave me a honey-do list. She asked that I get the laundry done. She gave me the grocery list. She told me about Aspen's nap time.

Then she started telling me about her grocery store routine, and very little of it had to do with shopping. Most of it had to do with Aspen: get the car cart, stop for a snack, make sure you have extra binkies . . .

The whole time I nodded, eyes glassy, face in my phone, paying little attention.

"You do realize you are taking Aspen grocery shopping alone, right? She's a psycho."

We were sitting at the dining room table. I'd spent long stretches of time with Aspen. I don't know if I'd ever spent all day with her, 100 percent alone, no backup. And I'd taken her to the store. But I hadn't ever taken her to the store for a full week's shopping trip alone, which would mean spending an hour wandering the grocery store aisles with a curious and disgruntled handful of a toddler. But I didn't really think about the reality of all that. I simply leaned on the fact that I was a dad and had been one for some time. Ten years, in fact. I could write an essay on parenting and publish it in the *New York Times*. I could manage a staff of 50 immature college-student employees. Surely I could take a two-year-old to the store alone, right?

I leaned back, folded my arms, and said, "She's my buddy. I've got this. I've been a father for how long now? Going to the store with one kid is nothing."

> I COULD WRITE AN ESSAY ON PARENTING AND PUBLISH IT IN THE *NEW YORK TIMES*. I COULD MANAGE A STAFF OF 50 IMMATURE COLLEGE-STUDENT EMPLOYEES. SURELY I COULD TAKE A TWO-YEAR-OLD TO THE STORE ALONE, RIGHT?

Part of the problem with all this was that I felt a little offended. It felt like Mel didn't trust me. And when I think back on that, I don't believe that's what Mel was getting at with her advice. I think she did trust me. That's why she was sending me. But she wanted me to learn from her mistakes. I think she felt like she was doing me a favor, but I came at her like I had this job down, and her advice wasn't needed, which ultimately made me look like a dick.

She scoffed.

Then she leaned forward, looked me in the eyes, and said, "She's going to destroy you."

I thought about those words as a young man named Steve, a tall, skinny black-haired store clerk in his late teens, helped me clean up the spaghetti sauce mess. He was pleasant about it, and I offered to pay for the sauce, but he refused. I apologized about a bazillion times. Near the end, as he was putting away the mop bucket, Aspen grabbed another bottle of sauce, this time Alfredo, and tried to throw it. Luckily, I grabbed her hand just in time, and Steve gave me that wide-eyed look that nonparents get when they witness the realities of a toddler. Then he snickered a bit and said, "She just doesn't care, does she?"

I didn't respond. I just pushed the cart into the next aisle.

That night, once everything was settled, the groceries were put away and the kids were in bed, I started complaining to Mel about my time at the store. I told her about the spaghetti sauce and the fits. I told her about how Aspen managed to get free from the seat buckle in an amazing escape worthy of Harry Houdini and almost tip the cart. Once I got her buckled again, she was eating a baguette. "I don't know where she got it, but she'd taken like four bites already so I had to buy it."

Mel nodded with arms folded in her lap as though she were a counselor of some sort, listening, processing and getting ready to deliver some hard reality about how I needed to change my lifestyle.

Then she smiled.

ALL SHE SAID WAS, "BRIBE HER."

It was the smirk she often gets when she feels that things are coming full circle. I'd walked in her shoes and realized that what I was dealing with was an altogether new form of parenting hell. However, she didn't lean forward and say, "I told you so." She didn't remind me of all the advice she'd tried to give me at the beginning to make my life easier, all the wisdom she'd learned from taking Aspen to the store week after week.

All she said was, "Bribe her."

I had a knee-jerk reaction right then, and I thought about all the discussions I'd read online about how bribery is rewarding bad behavior, and every time you go to the store your child knows that if they throw a fit they will get a treat. I thought about what my mother would say: "That's what's wrong with America. Kids are coddled and bribed into good behavior, and then they reach the real world and can't cope."

This isn't to say that I hadn't given my children a reward for good behavior at the store. I had. But what Mel went on to suggest was that I start off with a treat, give a treat near the middle, and stick to a rigid routine. This was exactly what she had told me before I took my first trip to the store, only this time I was actually listening.

"No," I said. "I'm not going to bribe her every time I go to the store. That's horrible parenting."

Mel laughed again. "Suit yourself. But every trip you take to the store with her and don't bribe her is going to be hell. Mark my words."

It was then that I laughed. "No way," I said. "I'm going to fix this. You know what? You and your bribery is probably what got us here in the first place. I hope you are proud of yourself. Now I have to clean up your mess."

Mel raised her eyebrows. Then she slapped my knee and said, "Good luck with that." She walked down the hall, her hips swinging just slightly, her posture almost too confident.

The next Saturday, I held strong. I sat Aspen down in the first cart I found. Not a car cart like Mel suggested originally, just a regular one. No frills, I thought. She arched her back up like I was trying to place her on a hot stove, her soft face bright red and frustrated. Then she tried to kick me in the crotch. She screamed, and passersby stared at me.

It was a pretty good workout, but I got her in.

She spent the next ten minutes or so screaming "I stuck. I stuck."

At one point we passed a car cart, and she pointed at it and screamed with desire; all the while I was trying very hard to find a good lime but couldn't concentrate, so I just threw some in a bag.

We hit the bulk section, and she screamed and reached for things, but I kept an eye on her. In fact, the first half of the trip, outside of fits, she didn't get into too much mischief.

But then there was a moment when I had my back turned and was looking for some pretzels that I got a sick feeling. It was really quiet, and for a moment I made a rookie mistake. I assumed that I'd won. That Aspen was being good at the store because she'd given up. My shape-up-or-ship-out attitude had won her over, and she was ready to be a quiet, well-behaved young girl growing into a successful adult.

This was the turning point, people.

I imagined myself being interviewed sometime in the future on some *20/20*-style program. They'd ask me when I knew my youngest daughter would sit on the Supreme Court, and I'd mention this very moment in the grocery store.

I turned around to see that in less than 5 minutes, Aspen had managed to reach behind her and empty half the cart of groceries. Bread, tortilla chips, carrots, heads of lettuce, boxes of cereal, really anything she could reach was on the floor. Above her head was an energy drink. It was something I needed to get through the rest of the day with her. Right before she slammed it to the ground, she looked at me with cold, glossy eyes that reminded me of The Undertaker before he pulled his signature tombstone wrestling move that was sure to knock out any opponent.

The drink hit the ground and exploded.

I found myself next to Steve again, the same store clerk who helped with the spaghetti sauce, as he mopped, and I apologized. He was as friendly as the last time, but there was something about the way he looked at me and then Aspen that seemed to show his true irritation.

RIGHT BEFORE SHE SLAMMED IT TO THE GROUND, SHE LOOKED AT ME WITH COLD, GLOSSY EYES THAT REMINDED ME OF THE UNDERTAKER BEFORE HE PULLED HIS SIGNATURE TOMBSTONE WRESTLING MOVE THAT WAS SURE TO KNOCK OUT ANY OPPONENT.

That night, once the kids were in bed, Mel sat next to me on the sofa and asked why all the produce was bruised and sticky and the tortilla chips looked like they'd been stomped on. I let out a long, agonizing breath that came from somewhere deep inside my body, near where I store all my deepest shame.

I told her what had happened at the store. I told her about Steve and how embarrassing it was to have the same clerk help me. She snuggled up next to me. She didn't say that she was sorry, and she didn't gloat. Instead she put her arm around me like she was consoling an old friend. She patted my shoulder, and it felt like she was saying, "You have hit bottom. Let's rebuild you. Make you stronger."

"How about I give you my advice once again about going to the store. We will go through it line by line."

She smiled at me, and I nodded, sheepishly.

"Get a car cart," she said. "A regular cart could get you killed. Next to the apples is a display of Fruit Roll-Ups. Give her one and pay for it later." She went on, telling me that the Fruit Roll-Up becomes, more or less, a ticking time bomb. I had until it was finished to get all the groceries on my list between the produce aisle and the bakery section (where they give free cookies to kids). If she's scraped that plastic liner clean of mashed fruit before we make it, she turns into a screaming, sticky-faced a-hole.

"It's not really about bribery," she said. "It's about keeping your sanity. And if that means a car cart, a Fruit Roll-Up and a cookie, then so be it."

That next Saturday I followed her directions to a T. I got the car cart. I picked up a Fruit Roll-Up. I went to the bakery. And as I was standing in line at the register, Aspen happily chomping away on a pink sugar cookie, I saw Steve in the distance. He was standing next to a grocery cart with a screaming brown-haired toddler in it. On the floor was a busted bottle of pickles, and standing nearby, apologizing, was a young father. I looked down at them, smiled and thought, "You should have listened to your wife."

Once I was in the van and the groceries were loaded, I sat in the driver's seat and looked back at Aspen. She'd fallen asleep in her car seat as I'd loaded the van. Her blond head leaned to the right, hands sticky with sugar cookie, face spackled in Fruit Roll-Up. I felt a warmth of satisfaction that only comes from making a successful trip to the store with a toddler.

I took a selfie with Aspen sleeping behind me, her face a mess, and our bags of groceries behind her. I sent it to Mel with the caption, "The store was a success! Your plan worked like a charm."

She responded with a kissy emoji. Then she wrote, "You're welcome."

25 THINGS PEOPLE DO DAILY THAT ARE MORE SHAMEFUL THAN BREASTFEEDING IN PUBLIC

The first time Mel had to breastfeed in a public restroom, I remember thinking it was odd. I mean, honestly, what could be more natural than breastfeeding? It's tried-and-true. Women have been doing it since the dawn of humankind. And, yet, there she was cramming our child into a dirty restroom stall as though breastfeeding was as shameful as public urination.

Before having children, I thought breastfeeding was not for public consumption. However, after having children, I know how wrong I was. I can't think of anything more wholesome and companionate than when Mel breastfed our children. And the more I think about that, the more I realize that there are actually a multitude of things that people do each day that are way more shameful than breastfeeding a child. Here's a list to give you an idea of what I'm talking about:

1. Popping zits while driving on the freeway using that little mirror on the sunshade (both gross and life threatening).

2. Arguing with your spouse in a restaurant.

3. Listening to Christmas music between Halloween and Thanksgiving.

4. Using breasts to sell cars, beer or any other product (I mean, honestly. What are breasts really designed for? Marketing or milk?).

5. Placing your entire mouth on the drinking fountain (Norah is a pro at this. We're working on it).

6. Picking your butt, nose and teeth (hopefully not in that order, but, you know, sometimes . . .).

7. Not washing your hands after using the restroom (my preschooler has that down).

8. Changing clothing for an interview in a parking lot (everyone can still see your doodle).

9. Taking your shoes and socks off while on a long plane ride and then cramming your naked feet between the seat and window so the person in front of you can see your nasty toes.

10. Looking a woman square in the chest rather than the eyes.

11. Chewing with your mouth open.

12. Scratching your junk while manspreading on the subway.

13. Riding on a city bus while chomping on a breakfast burrito dripping with grease, and then washing it all down with loud gulps from a massive fountain drink.

14. Wearing Crocs (the holes are where your dignity escapes).

15. Letting your crack hang out because a) your pants are too small, or b) you think it's sexy.

16. Talking on the phone while using a public restroom ("yeah" . . . grunt . . . "sure" . . . grunt . . . "we can come for dinner").

17. Being unnecessarily rude to anyone in a customer service position.

18. Cutting in line.

19. Anything that occurs on Black Friday.

20. Catcalling women (this makes me sick).

21. Screaming hillbilly-like threats at your child or spouse while shopping in a department store.

22. Drying your genitals with a hand dryer in the gym locker room.

23. Plucking chin hairs while eating fast food. (My grandma plucked her chin hairs with tweezers when we were eating hotcakes at McDonald's one time. I was ten. My therapist and I talk about it a lot.)

24. Spreading your butt cheeks apart on a chair so your fart doesn't make noise (not that I'd know anything about that . . .).

25. Judging mothers for breastfeeding in public.

Okay, so . . . in the name of full transparency, I have done at least half of these (I'll leave it up to you to guess which ones). But for the sake of mothers everywhere trying to find a dark hole to breastfeed their child, how about we cut them a little slack? How about we stop judging mothers for using their breasts for their intended purpose?

Because, honestly, we all do a lot of nasty things in public. Breastfeeding really shouldn't be considered one of them.

> **IF I HAD TO CHOOSE BETWEEN HAVING MY SON'S HELP AND SLAMMING MY HAND IN A CAR DOOR, I'D TAKE THE CAR DOOR**

I'd been laying sod in the backyard most of the day. We'd just moved into a white 1,000-square-foot home in a rural Oregon suburb. We were thrilled to have a yard, even if it was small. The woman who owned the house before us obviously hadn't had children, and she'd made some interesting choices in the backyard, most of them involving large patches of rocks that weren't good for kids to play on.

I was removing all those rocks and replacing them with grass and thinking about how I really should bring my son out to help. But here's the thing. This is the question all parents have to ask when thinking about getting their children to help with a project. If the kids help, will they actually be helping or just making a difficult project even more aggravating?

Two days earlier, I had asked Tristan to help pull weeds in the backyard, and he went boneless, fell on the floor and made this horrible noise that sounded like Chewbacca dying. He was eight, the oldest, so it had seemed like a good time to introduce him to yard work. He hadn't had much opportunity until that moment; we'd always lived in upstairs apartments until then.

I HAD ASKED TRISTAN TO HELP PULL WEEDS IN THE BACKYARD, AND HE WENT BONELESS, FELL ON THE FLOOR AND MADE THIS HORRIBLE NOISE THAT SOUNDED LIKE CHEWBACCA DYING.

I dragged him out into the yard, and he stood and looked at me with cold, tearful eyes.

"I don't care about the weeds," he said.

And I thought, *I don't care that you don't care about the weeds.* But I didn't know how to say that without bringing his morale down, so I just carried on, showing him how to pull the weeds. The project should have taken ten minutes but ended up taking 45; most of the extra time was spent arguing with my son and trying desperately to resist the urge to bury him in the garden.

Every project with Tristan "helping me" has been more about me redirecting him. Arguing with him. Trying desperately to keep him focused long enough to gain a work ethic. And I think what I really want is for Tristan to leave my house knowing how to work, but teaching him how to work felt like more work, and sometimes it feels like all I do is work.

I AM LEFT IMAGINING MY SON AS SOME PASTY TWENTY-SOMETHING WITH GREASY HAIR AND GLASSY EYES, LIVING IN MY BASEMENT, DIGGING INTO A BAG OF CHIPS AND PLAYING VIDEO GAMES RATHER THAN GOING TO COLLEGE, GETTING MARRIED AND GETTING THE HELL OUT OF MY HOUSE.

I mean, honestly, if I had a choice between having him help me with a project and slamming my hand in a car door, I'd take the car door. It would be less painful.

But then, right there, that's where the guilt comes in. That's where I am left imagining my son as some pasty twenty-something with greasy hair and glassy eyes, living in my basement, digging into a bag of chips and playing video games rather than going to college, getting married and getting the hell out of my house.

I thought about all of this as I looked at the yard, the sod and the piles of rocks.

I went into the house to find Tristan on his stomach in his room playing on a tablet. He was in black soccer shorts and a yellow Pokémon T-shirt.

"I need your help in the yard, bud," I said.

Then I braced myself for his complaining. I got ready for him to roll his eyes. To whine and argue with me. I told myself to keep calm.

I reached inside for my power animal.

REMEMBER, EARLIER IN THE STORY, WHEN I SAID I WANTED TO BURY MY SON IN THE GARDEN? WELL ... I HAD THAT URGE AGAIN.

Tristan rolled onto his back. Then he sat up and said, "I already helped Mom with the dishes. I'm not helping you in the yard. That's your job."

He let out a long, exhausted breath.

Then he said, "I have to do everything around here."

Remember, earlier in the story, when I said I wanted to bury my son in the garden? Well . . . I had that urge again.

My teenage niece once said something like this to my older brother. It was evening, so he went into the garage, turned off the main breaker to the house and went to bed. As he passed her room, he said, "If you have to do everything around here, you can start paying the power bill."

It was a bold move on his part.

I was proud of him.

I thought about doing something similar, but Mel was cooking.

I like to think that I wasn't this difficult as a child, but I'm sure I was. I'm confident that every time my parents asked me to do anything outside of watching *The Price Is Right* and eating gummy worms I looked at them like they were sentencing me to an internment camp. I have to assume that this struggle is universal. I don't think my son is abnormal here, nor do I think that I'm doing anything wrong. But, ultimately, knowing this doesn't make trying to get my son to work any less irritating.

I sat down next to Tristan, and he looked at me with straight white lips, like he was ready for a fight.

I wanted to say, "Who do you think you are, bub?" I wanted to lay into him. I wanted to tell him to stop acting like helping with the dishes or the yard was some great favor to his mother and father.

I wanted to ground his little butt.

But I didn't. Instead, I took a breath and said, "Do you know how much I work each week?"

He shrugged like he didn't care.

I told him that I worked two jobs, one at the university and the other as a freelance writer. "When I'm not working to make money, I'm working to care for our home or to teach you and your sisters how to become good kids. All I do is work. And do you know who I work for?"

He shrugged.

"It's not only for Mom, and it's not only for me, and it's not only for you or you sisters. It's for our family. It's for all of us."

I told him how I was working in the yard so that our family would have a place to play. "When you were doing dishes earlier," I said. "That wasn't for Mom. That's not her job. And working in the yard, that's not my job. It's our job. This is our family. No one is cleaning for Mom, and no one is working for Dad. We are all in this together, so stop complaining and pitch in."

He looked up at me with soft eyes, and for a moment I assumed we were having one of those *Leave It to Beaver* moments, where the father says just the right thing, and the Beaver changes his mind about everything. I expected him to smile, apologize and then walk outside and work without complaint.

That was stupid.

Instead he rolled his eyes and said, "Whatever" in an exacerbated, put out, everything sucks kind of voice. Then he walked out of his room and into the yard.

Together we worked for two hours. He complained most of the time, which was expected. I had to redirect him about a million times. That was expected, too. But once the sod was down and we had the sprinklers on, I put a sweaty dirty arm around my sweaty dirty son and said, "It's going to be pretty cool to play soccer with you back here."

He looked up at me with a smile.

"Yeah," he said.

I crouched down so I could look him in the eyes. Then I said, "There was a time when I used to think that doing things around the house was for your mother. But I was wrong. I was helping out the family. In a lot of ways, I was helping out myself. It's kind of the same thing here. You helped in the yard, and now we can play soccer back here. You weren't helping me. You were helping the family. Doesn't it feel good to help the family?"

He shrugged again, and I wondered if I still hadn't gotten through to him. I wondered how many more times I would have to teach him this lesson.

Once we were finished he said, "Yeah. I guess it feels okay."

It wasn't exactly enthusiastic, but it was better than when we started, so I felt like I'd had a small victory.

I GRUDGINGLY LET MY SON BLOW ALL HIS MONEY

Tristan had his tenth birthday party and ended up with a whopping 50 dollars in cash and gift cards, making him basically a millionaire. He asked me to take him to the store so he could buy a video game, and I'll be honest. I wasn't 100 percent on board with it.

I wanted him to make the adult decision and save his money.

I made suggestions on what he could save it for: college, family, retirement . . . I even suggested investing in stocks. When I was his age, I remember blowing all my birthday money on a copy of *Street Fighter 2* for Sega Genesis. I played that game like crazy for a few months. Then it got old, and

I moved on. Had I invested that money in, say, Microsoft, I'd probably be a happier and wealthier man now. I mentioned all of this to him, and he gave me an epic eye roll as though I'd suggested he light the money on fire.

HE WAS BALDING AND HAD THAT "I WORK AT A VIDEO GAME STORE; THIS HAS ALWAYS BEEN MY LIFE GOAL" DISPOSITION.

Nothing I proposed was particularly sexy or exciting, so we ended up in front of the Walmart video game case, looking for some Pokémon game that I can't pronounce or spell. The game wasn't on the shelf, so I had to coach him through asking the store clerk. He was a man in his late twenties with tattoos of the Mario Brothers and game consoles on his arms. He was balding and had that "I work at a video game store; this has always been my life goal" disposition.

He was the kind of guy I probably would have looked up to at the age of ten, but now, as a father, I hope my son strives for larger aspirations.

I mean, nothing too grandiose.

I just want Tristan to be a rock star father and the next CEO of a Fortune 500 company.

Or an astronaut.

Or the president of the United States.

Or all three. Is that too much to ask?

Last week, he scored two goals in his peewee soccer game, and he once made a robot out of Post-It notes. Obviously the boy has huge, massive, potential.

A good savings account along with some wise investments could set him up for major success.

Right?

I say this like I have a savings account. I mean, I sometimes do. Sometimes we have money in the bank. Sometimes a medical bill or broken-down vehicle doesn't bleed me dry.

I SAY THIS LIKE I HAVE A SAVINGS ACCOUNT. I MEAN, I SOMETIMES DO. SOMETIMES WE HAVE MONEY IN THE BANK.

Here's the thing: I think a lot of fathers feel this way about their sons, and that's why when Tristan got a wad of cash on his birthday, I advised him to spend it wisely. I advised him on all the ways I could have done this or that better with my money, because I am old enough to look back and wonder if I actually reached my full potential. Perhaps I could have been a CEO if I'd invested that *Street Fighter* money.

Who knows; maybe even the president.

Or an astronaut.

Or all three.

Maybe if I'd saved that money, I wouldn't have to buy those discounted off-brand work polos that fit like a poncho, or that off-brand cereal on the bottom shelf that tastes pretty good, but also sometimes tastes like struggling to make ends meet.

Am I being too dramatic?

Probably.

Tristan stood next to the register, anxiously tapping the toes of the beat-up Nikes he's refused to throw away, half a smile on his face, his hair a little messy in the back, some white dried-up birthday cake frosting on the front of his jacket.

> MAYBE IF I'D SAVED THAT MONEY, I WOULDN'T HAVE TO BUY THOSE DISCOUNTED OFF-BRAND WORK POLOS THAT FIT LIKE A PONCHO, OR THAT OFF-BRAND CEREAL ON THE BOTTOM SHELF THAT TASTES PRETTY GOOD, BUT ALSO SOMETIMES TASTES LIKE STRUGGLING TO MAKE ENDS MEET.

I thought about how two years earlier, when Tristan was eight, I actually went as far as to take him to the bank the day after his birthday, and make him put 20 percent of his birthday money in savings. "It's just 20 percent, buddy. If you save

20 percent of your income for the rest of your life, you will be set for retirement."

He looked up at me with turned-down lips.

During the whole drive to the bank, he held on to a birthday envelope of cash with a white-knuckle grip, his face soft and white as though I were taking him someplace really dreadful. It was a short drive, not more than about ten minutes, and on the way there, he asked me more than once if he "had to."

I TRIED TO MAKE SAVING MONEY SOUND EXCITING. IT WASN'T TAKING ...

"Yes," I said. "Absolutely. Saving money is the best thing you can do." I tried to make saving money sound exciting.

It wasn't taking, and I wondered if I was doing it wrong.

Once we got to the counter to make a deposit, he had a look of dread on his face, as if I'd eaten all his cake in front of him.

That moment at the bank was in stark contrast to the moment at the video game store. And, sure, it probably should be. Buying a game as a little boy is way more exciting than saving money. Hell, it's more exciting as an adult. There's something so gratifying about getting a little money and then blowing it on something stupid at the store. And although I really wanted to force him to save the money and show him the importance of a fat savings account, I totally understood why he was at the store, excitedly waiting for the clerk to come back with some silly thing that won't matter in six months.

I've often heard people say, "Nothing in life is a sure thing." But is that actually true? Because the reality is that Tristan blowing all of his birthday money on that game was a surefire ticket to a happy little boy. And I must admit there is something pretty priceless about that. And maybe that was the real rub in this situation . . . as a father, I could see both sides. Part of me wanted Tristan to do the responsible thing and save his money, but another part longed to feel the thrill of being a little boy again, blowing all his birthday money at Walmart.

This whole dad and son thing, it's a two-way street. My job as a father is to teach him responsibility, to love him and guide him and hope for the best. His job is to live and learn, sometimes from my advice, and sometimes through trial and error.

Suggesting my son spend his money wisely, that's what fathers do. If it doesn't take, I'll try again. And again. Worst case scenario, I'll get to say, "I told you so."

I did my part.

Now it was his time to shine.

Tristan grinned from ear to ear when the clerk came back with the game. This might have been the best day of his life.

We bought it. He opened it in the car and told me all about how cool it was. I listened. I asked questions. We laughed. And the moment we got home, I pulled the ultimate fatherly move by making him clean his room before he could play.

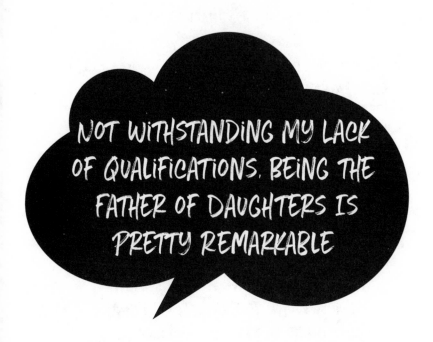

NOT WITHSTANDING MY LACK OF QUALIFICATIONS, BEING THE FATHER OF DAUGHTERS IS PRETTY REMARKABLE

When the sonographer told us we were having a girl, I said, "Are you sure you're using that right?"

Mel was in a hospital bed, slightly inclined, her pregnant stomach pushing out beneath her shirt and covered in clear medical jelly.

She punched me in the arm.

I was 25, and this was our second child. My question was supposed to be a joke, but there was some truth to what I said. I have one sister, and she's seven years older than me. She felt more like a second mother than a sister. I hadn't spent much time around little girls, so when I did, they seemed screechy and strange. Our son, Tristan, already made a lot of sense, and the thought of having

215

another boy felt comfortable. But with a girl, I honestly didn't know what to expect. I remember looking at the blurry black-and-white image of our baby. I was pretty sure what I was looking at were hips, but with a sonogram, I can almost never tell. Those things always look like a black-and-white video of something moving inside a bowl of pasta.

There was an arrow pointing on the screen, and below it was written, Girl.

BUT WITH IT BEING A GIRL, I DIDN'T KNOW WHAT TO EXPECT, AND THAT CAUSED ME TO FEEL REALLY UNCERTAIN. WHEN I SAY UNCERTAIN I ACTUALLY MEAN TERRIFIED.

I wondered what it means to be the father of a daughter. And when I thought about that question, I got really scared. Becoming a father the first time was terrifing because I didn't have much of a father myself. But once Mel was pregnant a second time, I felt more confident. I felt like I could handle a second child. But with it being a girl, I didn't know what to expect, and that caused me to feel really uncertain.

When I say *uncertain* I actually mean *terrified*.

But now, looking back, if I've learned anything about being the father of a daughter it's that it means feeling underqualified. It means a melted heart. It means reading a poorly written book that summarizes the movie *Frozen* every night for six weeks, and although the writing is terrible and I'm sick of the story, I do it because few things are sweeter than having my daughter snuggled next to me. It means driving to work at 6:00 a.m., alone, and somehow finding myself singing "Let It Go." It means looking at Barbie and wondering if she is setting a bad example of beauty for my daughter. It means looking at Norah's blue-green eyes and realizing that she has as much power over me as I have over her.

When Norah was almost two, she accidently stuck her right hand in a bowl of 400-degree, oven-baked mashed potatoes. She cried loud and hard, and as I sat next to that sweet, chubby-cheeked little girl in the emergency room, listening to her deep wail as the nurse peeled away her soft, dead skin, I cried harder than I did after my father's death. How could I have anticipated that surge of emotion? I'd never wanted to take someone's pain away until then. I'd never felt that before, and, honestly, I never want to feel it again. I wanted Norah to be whole. I wanted her to be sweet and wonderful forever. In that emergency room, I never wanted her to feel pain ever again. I felt the strongest need to protect her. And yet this moment was evidence that I wouldn't always be able to protect her. She would get hurt again someday, and that meant I would hurt, too.

When she had a crush on a young boy at church, I couldn't help but look at him and think, "Norah. You can do better." The moment that thought crossed my mind, I was struck with the age-old question that seems to hit most fathers: Who is good enough for my daughter? I got the answer almost immediately. "No one." Yet I knew that she would one day meet someone and fall in love, and somehow I was going to have to deal with that, and I didn't know how.

IT MEANT KNOWING THAT SHE WILL GROW UP TO BE A STRONG-WILLED WOMAN BUT REALIZING THAT MEANS PUTTING UP WITH A STRONG-WILLED LITTLE GIRL WITH AN ASSHOLE FACE.

Having a daughter meant a mix of new emotions that for me, as a man, were completely unexpected. It meant realizing that I, indeed, had a soft side. It meant I wasn't all that tough. It meant realizing nothing is as gratifying as the words, "I *wove* you, Daddy," and no words stung worse than, "I'm never ever going to talk to you ever again!"

It meant knowing that she will grow up to be a strong-willed woman but realizing that means putting up with a strong-willed little girl with an asshole face. That's where Norah tilts her head to the side, makes eye contact and draws her lips in to a straight line. Then she does whatever I just told her not to. I tell her not to drink more water before bed, and she gives me the asshole face—and drinks more water. Once, at one of Tristan's basketball games, Mel told Norah not to go into the other court with her friend, and Norah turned, gave her the asshole face and kept walking.

Every time she gives me the asshole face, I tell her to cut the crap. "Don't look at me like that," I say. "Who do you think you are?" And sure enough, she does it anyway.

I tell her not to talk back, and she says, "You can't talk to a princess like that." And the really frustrating part is, according to her schoolteachers, Norah is reserved and soft-spoken when at school. While I will admit that I was happy to find this out, part of me wonders if she is only snarky at home because she secretly hates her parents.

I know this all seems overly complicated. I am her father. I should have the power to make her do what I tell her. I am the giver of food, clothing and shelter. But the sad reality is that my kids have just as much control over me as I do over them, and I suspect that Norah fully understands this. I can see it in her eyes. I can see it in the cock of her head. I can see it in the way she hugs me and whispers sweet nothings in my ear.

When I complain about my daughter to other parents, they always say, "Just wait until she's a teen." And suddenly I think of when I was a teen and how my teen friends complained about their parents, and how, at the time, something as simple as a curfew seemed unjust. And suddenly I feel like there is no hope.

It's in these dark, frustrating parenting moments that I try to think about the small parenting victories. I think about the times when Norah sits on my lap, and I help her with her homework. I think about the bright gap-toothed smile on her face when she figures out how to read a long complicated word, and she immediately seeks out my approval. I think about times when she calls me at work to tell me about getting an award at school. Every once in a while I get a glimpse of her becoming who I know she can be—a bright, responsible adult. A strong woman and a passionate, loving daughter and sibling.

With our third child, Mel had another ultrasound. Sure enough, we were having another girl. Tristan was seven at the time, and he asked if we could change it to a boy, whereas Norah, age five, smiled from ear to ear at the thought of having a baby sister.

I thought about the drive to the ultrasound. Norah sang "Let It Go" in her sweet five-year-old voice. My heart melted like it always does when Norah sings. Sure, Norah was complicated. But so was my son at times. But despite my lack of qualifications, Norah was turning into a sweet, wonderful little girl, and I had all the faith in the world that she'd grow into a wonderful woman someday. And when I thought about that, I didn't feel scared at all to have another girl. In fact, I felt excited. I couldn't believe I was so anxious in the first place. I realized I had no reason to be afraid of being the father of a daughter, and I was wrong to be scared. Sure, Norah was frustrating sometimes. But so are all kids, regardless of gender.

I looked down at Norah. She had a huge smile. I crouched down and said, "You are going to be a big sister. Are you excited?"

She nodded enthusiastically. Then she said, "She'll get to have you as a daddy."

Then she clapped.

I paused for a moment. I didn't expect her to say that, but at the time it was exactly what I needed to hear.

"Yes," I said. "Yes, she will."

ALL THE THINGS I NEVER SHOULD'VE SAID AFTER OUR FIRST CHILD (NOT A COMPREHENSIVE LIST)

I was 24 when we had our first child. I had no idea what I was doing. I was young and scared and it caused me to say some really bonehead things to Mel. I feel horrible about it, so, once again, I am going to have a conversation with my former self. Hopefully you new fathers out there can learn from my mistakes.

"WHEN DID THE DOCTOR SAY WE COULD HAVE SEX AGAIN?"

Oh, poor you. Having to go a few months without sex. Your wife just had a six-pound baby ripped from a gaping hole in her stomach, but how horny you are pales in comparison to your wife's C-section. Dude . . . deal with it. Your wife just grew a baby inside her body, then had a major surgery where a human life was dragged out of her and then she was crudely stapled back together. Do you really think she needs you crammed up inside her? Think with your head for a minute. Give her body a rest. She's earned it.

'THERE IS NO REASON THE BABY SHOULD BE SLEEPING IN OUR BED!' Oh stop being all territorial. Getting up in the night sucks, and a mother only gets a very short time to snuggle with a baby. If she wants that child in the bed, let it happen. It will be over soon enough, and you'll go back to serenading only your wife with your snoring and farts.

'WHEN ARE WE GOING TO START EXERCISING AGAIN?' I see what you did there. You said *we*, not *you*. Classy. You know what your wife just heard? "You need to get busy losing that baby weight." Or maybe, "I'm not finding you as attractive after having a baby." So basically you just confirmed what most women fear after having a child. Nice work, dickhead. You are both adjusting to a new baby. She is adjusting to a new baby *and* a new body. You married her because she is sweet and wonderful. Because she made you feel like a better man. Not simply because she looked good in a pair of jeans. So think about that and give the new mom a break. She will start working out when *she's* ready. You worry about your body.

'THE BABY CAN'T BE THAT SICK. HE DOESN'T NEED TO SEE A DOCTOR.' I get it. Money is tight. You just had a baby. But you have insurance with a decent deductible. What your wife wants right now is peace of mind because the thought of losing a child because you didn't take him to the doctor is probably the scariest thing in the history of ever. Eventually your wife will figure out that doctors can't do crap for a child under two, but until that happens, just shut up and take the kid to the doctor. It'll be fine.

'UGH ... DO I HAVE TO CHANGE THE BABY?' Yes you do! You are a dad! This is a partnership. If the baby is poopy, handle it. Don't pass that crap onto your wife. Take pride in it. This is a new era. An egalitarian age when a man can change a diaper and feel good about it. Take advantage of the fact that with the simple act of changing a baby's diaper without complaint you can be a huge help to your growing family. Stop being lazy and stop acting like you are better than the job. Own it!

'STOP BUYING SO MANY BABY OUTFITS. HE'S NOT GOING TO GROW OUT OF THINGS THAT FAST. I THINK YOU JUST WANT TO SPEND MONEY.' Listen here. Babies grow at the same pace as chia pets. It's incredible. The problem isn't that your wife likes to spend money, so stop putting the blame on her. She actually took the time to read a couple of parenting books and learned how quickly children grow out of every single thing. She's planning ahead. Stop being uninformed. Stop being cheap. Start enjoying the moment.

'THERE'S NO REASON FOR ME TO GET UP AT NIGHT. YOU ARE THE ONE WITH THE FOOD.' Huge cop-out, dude. Your wife had the child. You saw it, and it freaked you out. Now she's producing food for the child, so you think thrusting all nighttime duties on her is justified. Cut the crap. The baby's diaper still needs to be changed at night. The baby still needs to be rocked to sleep, tucked in and snuggled with. Sometimes laundry needs to be done at night when things get messy. There are plenty of things that happen during the night outside of feeding, so step it up and stop trying to get out of your obligations.

'HOW LONG DO YOU THINK YOU'LL HAVE THOSE STRETCH MARKS?' This just in, you need to think before you speak, jackass. She's going to have them forever, and that's not a bad thing. Those stretch marks are a sign that she was dedicated enough to change her body permanently to bring your squirmy poop-filled baby into the world. How about you stop looking at them like they are blemishes, and start looking at them as signs of dedication.

Okay. Okay. I've probably been a little hard on myself, but maybe that's a good thing. Now I just hope some of you awesome fathers out there can learn from my mistakes. Let's be supportive, dads. Let's start a new trend.

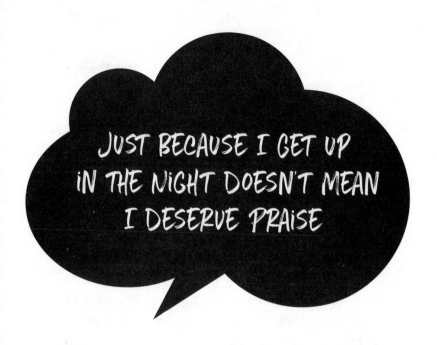

JUST BECAUSE I GET UP IN THE NIGHT DOESN'T MEAN I DESERVE PRAISE

I was chatting with Mel about the long night we'd had getting up with the baby when I said, "At least I get up with her. A lot of men don't. You should be grateful." I was tired. And I said it like she was really lucky to have me. Like I was going above and beyond as a father.

It was just after 7:00 a.m. With Aspen sleeping in her lap, Mel looked up at me. She was in the living room of our small home, sitting on a blue love seat stained by seven years of kids. Her eyes were a little red, and her brown hair was in a loose ponytail. She held the baby a little closer and took in what I had said. I expected her to agree with me. We sometimes talked about the fathers we knew who didn't get up with their babies. They viewed it as the mother's job.

She didn't agree with my statement.

Not even a little bit.

Instead, Mel crossed her legs, looked me in the eyes, and said, "I wish you'd stop saying that."

At the time, Mel was a nearly full-time college student, a mother of three and a school volunteer (a requirement of our children's charter school). She spent hours sitting at our kitchen table hunched over a keyboard, a textbook to her right, and at least one child tugging at her pant leg. And despite her commitment to education and how much I pitched in, she often commented on the pressure she felt to keep a clean house—not to mention take the children to the doctor, cook meals, shuttle the kids to sports and other extracurricular activities, keep them looking clean and healthy and monitor their behavior in public. She was a student and a mother, and yet she felt an enormous pressure to be the sole caregiver of our children. And there I was, feeding into those expectations by mentioning my help in the night as if it were some generous extension of my role as a father.

Naturally, I didn't think about any of this at the time. Instead, I thought about how gracious I was. How kind it was for me to get up in the night, like I deserved an honorary doctorate in awesomeness.

I was dressed in slacks and a collared shirt. In my right hand was a purple bag with my lunch. I paused for a moment, took a step back and said, "Why? I mean, it's true. I do a lot of stuff that other fathers don't. I'm a good guy."

I am a good guy. I can say that, right? I'm a dedicated father and husband. I do a lot of things most men don't. I was grocery shopping with my mother a while back while Mel was at home studying. In the cart were all three kids. As we walked through the aisles, my mother asked why I was shopping. The conversation soon led to how I often get up in the middle of the night with the kids and do the laundry, too. She just didn't understand where I came from, considering my father didn't do anything like that when I was young.

He went to work, brought in the check and came home. And he only did that for a few years until he walked out on us. I remember chatting with Mel once about her own father and how he refused to get up in the night with his children, along with change diapers or do any cooking outside of flipping burgers on the barbeque. Sadly, the "I bring home the bacon—anything else is extra and deserves praise" status quo still lingered in my subconscious.

Mel was standing now, the baby in her arms, her baggy blue pajama bottoms loose around her hips, the pant legs wedged beneath the heels of her gray slippers. Our older two children were still sleeping, so we spoke in whispers.

"When you say that, it doesn't make me feel like we're in a partnership," she spoke in a forced angry whisper. The kind of frustrated tone she often used when our children acted out in church. "It makes me feel like you want me to kiss your butt every time you get up in the night. This is your baby, too."

We went back and forth for a while. She told me how she appreciated all that I do around the house, but she hated the way I acted like I deserved a special pat on the back.

"I do way more than my father ever did," I said, all the while giving her a straight-lipped matter-of-fact look.

I did that a lot, actually, compared myself to my father, a man who walked out on my mother when I was nine years old. In so many ways it's easy to be better than him, but the reality is, comparing myself to a man who abandoned his children and died from drug and alcohol abuse is setting the bar pretty low.

Mel didn't have to tell me any of that, however. She just looked at me with slanted, cold glossy red eyes.

My knee-jerk reaction was to defend myself.

I wanted to give her a list of other fathers we knew, family and friends, who still subscribed to antiquated notions of gender roles. I wanted to list all my wonderfulness to justify why I didn't deserve to be treated like this.

At this point we'd been together for eleven years. We'd shared many life changes that come with marriage and family, and so if anyone was qualified to tell me that I was being a jackass, it was my wife.

Naturally I didn't think about that. Instead, I opened my mouth to dig the hole a little deeper but stopped, thought and decided to leave before I said something I shouldn't.

I walked out without saying a word.

I drove to work angry.

I mumbled under my breath.

I felt picked on.

NATURALLY I DIDN'T THINK ABOUT THAT. INSTEAD, I OPENED MY MOUTH TO DIG THE HOLE A LITTLE DEEPER ...

I was 20 minutes into my 30-minute commute before I started to calm down and really think about what Mel had said: " . . . it doesn't make me feel like we're in a partnership" and "This is your baby, too."

I thought about the last time I washed dishes. I'd assumed that I should be getting praise or a reward, and for the first time I asked myself, why? I ate there, too. Then I thought about vacuuming the carpet or doing the laundry and realized I had the same expectations about those chores, and suddenly I felt like a dickhead.

I was placing myself on a pedestal for doing things that Mel did every single day without complaint or any request for praise.

And once again, I thought about my father. He never had a rewarding conversation about hygiene with his son after doing his laundry. He never had the opportunity to discuss toast-cutting options with his daughter, and then moments later laugh his head off at how ridiculous a child can be at breakfast time. He never bathed a toddler and had her reach up from the tub and wash his face, her little blue-green eyes focused and adorable.

I THOUGHT ABOUT THE LAST TIME I WASHED DISHES. I'D ASSUMED THAT I SHOULD BE GETTING PRAISE OR A REWARD, AND FOR THE FIRST TIME I ASKED MYSELF, WHY?

He missed out on *all* the good stuff, those moments that I think about when I'm alone at work and suddenly can't stop smiling or laughing or feeling that warm tenderness in my chest that only comes from thinking about my kids.

He missed out on being a father.

And the more I thought about that, the more I realized that nothing I did for my family should be about praise.

It's about parenthood.

Dads are parents, too, and the rewards I needed to be worried about receiving from working in a partnership shouldn't come from my wife. They should come from the heartwarming everyday tender moments of being a committed, loving and dedicated father.

By the time I parked and walked to my office, I felt really low.

I knew that I needed to apologize, but I didn't want to. I never do even when I know it's the right thing to do. There's something awkward about an apology. There is humility in it that makes me feel nervous and uncertain and vulnerable.

But I knew I owed Mel an apology, so once I reached my office, I closed the door, called home and told her I was sorry. "You're right," I said. "This is a partnership, and I shouldn't act like I'm doing some amazing thing because I get up at night. I'm going to stop."

Mel didn't tell me about all the other times I'd acted this way. She didn't gloat or tell me that she wasn't ready to forgive me. She didn't say anything for what seemed like a long time but was probably only a short while.

Then she said, "Thank you."

MY KiDS WiLL NEVER ACT LiKE THAT (HOW WRONG I WAS)

I was in our minivan with a screaming toddler while the rest of the family finished their meals at Red Robin. It was dusk. The lights were off in the van, and Aspen was strapped into her car seat, her face soft and round and red, her little legs kicking. Her blond hair was pulled into adorable pigtails, and where her hair parted, her scalp was the same frustrated beet red as her face. I didn't lean between the seats to try to comfort her. I wasn't ready for that yet. I was pretty pissed off, so I just sat in the front seat and let her cry while I calmed down.

We didn't eat out all that much. Mostly because of money. We are a family of five, and Mel and I both work in education. But part of it was because of our toddler. She was so sweet and wonderful and curious and cute, but she was also two, which made her about as predictable and ill-tempered as a wild honey badger.

We'd been shopping in another town for most of the day. Once we finished up, it was a little after 6:00 p.m., and the kids were hungry, so we went out.

SHE WAS SO SWEET AND WONDERFUL AND CURIOUS AND CUTE, BUT SHE WAS ALSO TWO, WHICH MADE HER ABOUT AS PREDICTABLE AND ILL-TEMPERED AS A WILD HONEY BADGER.

We went to Red Robin because it was a middle ground kind of place, not actually nice, but sort of nice, with a bunch of crazy crap on the walls and overpriced mac 'n' cheese. You laugh, but mac 'n' cheese is pretty critical to parents of small children. In fact, if you are worried about parenting, buy mac 'n' cheese. Don't fight it. Just buy the hell out of that shit.

It'll be fine.

Anyway, Aspen refused to sit down. She flipped over the salt and pepper shakers. She snagged the drink menu and tried to rip it. Mel or I stopped her each time moments before too much damage was done, and each time she grew more frustrated, saying, *no* or *mine*. Once the food came, she threw chicken fingers at Tristan and laughed and laughed. Then she crawled under the table so she could sneak away to a candy-and-toy claw machine that sat in a far corner of the restaurant. Mel snagged her mid-escape, and Aspen screamed and screamed, and kicked and kicked, and since I was the only one finished with my salad, I had the pleasure of dragging her out to the van.

YOU LAUGH, BUT MAC 'N' CHEESE IS PRETTY CRITICAL TO PARENTS OF SMALL CHILDREN. IN FACT, IF YOU ARE WORRIED ABOUT PARENTING, BUY MAC 'N' CHEESE. DON'T FIGHT IT. JUST BUY THE HELL OUT OF THAT SHIT.

I carried her under my right arm, still kicking, still screaming like a miniature Trump protester. I lugged her past the bar, and everyone stared at me. *Everyone.* The young, hip black-haired bartender. The backward-hatted 30-something cool guy, hitting on the tightly-dressed blond. The three dudes wearing college sports apparel splitting a pitcher of locally brewed beer.

Most of them childless, I assumed. No one with children would give me that straight-faced, lip-twisted look that seems to say, "If you can't control your kid, then don't go out."

The hostess, a redhead in her late teens, opened the door for me as I hauled Aspen out. She gave me the same look as the others, and I wanted to look her straight in her smug stuck up little face and say, "Screw you. This is parenting. Deal with it."

Part of me wanted to walk back in, stand up on one of those bar tables, hold up my screaming toddler, and say, "Take a good look! This was you once. Cut me some slack, you stupid drunk yuppies!"

But I didn't because, you know, that would be rude and over the top and worthy of a Facebook live stream. As a grown man I'm supposed to be better than that, right?

But I didn't want to be.

I loaded Aspen into her car seat, fighting and screaming the whole time. All I could think about were those people in the bar. *For crying out loud*, I thought. *Aspen is two and it is going to take years to teach her how to act appropriately in public. Don't they understand that?*

Obviously not.

I crawled into the front seat and thought about how I used to think the same way they did.

Seven years earlier, when Tristan was three, I was shopping with him at a Target in Minnesota.

I was 26 and a young father and husband attending graduate school. Tristan was basically the mascot of my graduate program, and it was with good reason. He was the cutest, stockiest little boy, with big blue eyes and auburn hair.

He wore coveralls that day, with light-up fire trucks on his sneakers and a red T-shirt. He refused to sit in a cart, so I held his hand as we walked through the store.

He kept reaching out for things, and I kept stopping him. Eventually, he tugged on the arm of a dress, and almost pulled the rack over.

I don't know what it is about the strength of a toddler, but his grip was epic. If that dress were the sword in the stone, he'd become the king of England.

Somehow I broke his grip, and he melted down. He went nuclear.

> I DON'T KNOW WHAT IT IS ABOUT THE STRENGTH OF A TODDLER, BUT HIS GRIP WAS EPIC. IF THAT DRESS WERE THE SWORD IN THE STONE, HE'D BECOME THE KING OF ENGLAND.

He sprawled out on the floor, face and neck as red as his T-shirt, and screamed, the lights on his shoes flashing with each kick of his short frustrated legs.

What I remember best were the glares. The rolled eyes and irritated, put-out expressions from twenty-somethings who attended the same college I did. They were the same looks I got at Red Robin the day I hauled out Aspen.

One young woman said to her boyfriend, "If you can't control your kids, then stay home."

It felt like I needed to have better control over Tristan. Perhaps I should've been teaching him more at home and avoided taking him out until I was 100 percent sure he was ready. It felt like him throwing a fit was breaking some unwritten law of social decency.

But honestly, control a two-year-old? Sure, whatever. While I'm at it, why don't I go ahead and control the elements?

Or the stars.

Or the Kardashians.

It wasn't possible, and yet that day Tristan threw a fit in Target, I felt shame crawl up into my chest—hot and nasty.

BUT HONESTLY, CONTROL A TWO-YEAR-OLD? SURE, WHATEVER. WHILE I'M AT IT, WHY DON'T I GO AHEAD AND CONTROL THE ELEMENTS?

I was eager to right the situation, as if there is ever a way to right a toddler fit. I bent down to pick up my screaming son to take him to the car, and he punched me in the crotch.

Right in the money zone.

Then he laughed at me.

I buckled over, a pain in my gut, hands on my knees.

Tristan put his hands over his little tummy and laughed hard at my reaction. Long childlike laughter that reminded me of a grade-school bully.

I looked around, and, naturally, more people were watching. The same young woman who made the snarky remark earlier had her hand over her mouth in shock, and her expression seemed to say that I'd gotten what I deserved.

Once I stopped hurting, I swept Tristan up and carried him to the back of the store and into one of the dressing rooms. I stood him up on a chair and then crouched down so I could look him in the eyes.

Tristan stood there, one hand cradled in the other, his face a mix of fear and confusion, and I realized that he honestly had no idea that he'd done something wrong. I tried to put it in terms that he'd understand. I told him that what he'd done had hurt Daddy and made him sad. I could tell that he was listening. When working with a three-year-old, this is a huge accomplishment.

I honestly thought I was getting somewhere.

Then he picked his nose and ate it.

I let out a long breath.

I looked at the ground.

He dug into his nose for some more and then held out his finger, offering me a taste.

It was then, in that dressing room, that I realized I hadn't taught him that it was acceptable to throw a fit in a store, punch his father in the crotch and then laugh at him.

But at the same time, I never taught him that this *wasn't* okay.

Sometimes Tristan was like a car without a steering wheel, driving at full speed into this or that. I never really knew what he was going to do, and it took me a while to abandon logic and expect the unexpected.

I realized that there was no way for me to anticipate every random, crazy thing he was going to do in public, and it was going to take years to teach Tristan how to act appropriately. It was going to take a lot of frustrating, unexpected situations where I'd have to correct him on the fly. The only way I was ever going to teach him was to take him out and show him what was right and wrong. By saying no a million times, letting him throw a fit and telling him no again.

And every single one of these lessons was going to be in front of an audience of gawking jerks.

Flash forward, now I'm a father of three, and Tristan is a well-behaved young man. He sits quietly at restaurants, and he acts appropriately in stores, and he has done so for years.

In fact, he hasn't even offered me a booger in some time, although, I will admit, he still picks his nose and eats it.

We are working on that one.

I thought about what a good kid Tristan is

now as I sat in our dark minivan parked outside Red Robin, a screaming two-year-old Aspen in the back. I was attempting to wash away that feeling of shame that all parents get when a child throws a fit in a public place, and focus on the fact that I'd just taught my daughter a handful of very valuable lessons on the road to becoming a functioning person: don't throw food, don't scream in public, sit in your chair, listen to your parents . . .

Eventually, Aspen stopped screaming. She settled into her car seat, her lip still trembling a bit, eyes moist, boogers draining from her nose.

I turned around and looked at her.

We were both calmer now.

"Someday," I said while pointing at her. "You are going to figure out how to act in public. And once you do, I expect a thank you."

Aspen looked me in the eyes and started crying again.

I PAID FOR A PRINCESS
MAKEOVER BUT NOW
HAVE NO REGRETS

I was on Space Mountain when Mel took Norah to
the Bibbidi Bobbidi Boutique near Sleeping Beauty's
Castle at Disneyland. No one would ride Space
Mountain with me, so I went alone, which was kind
of a big deal, actually. My father died fifteen years
earlier on that same month. A year before he left my
mother, when I was eight, we took a family vacation
to Disneyland. The first roller-coaster I ever rode
was Space Mountain. My father insisted that I go,
even though I was terrified. He was in and out of
my life after my parents' divorce. Sometimes we'd
go a year or more without communication. That
ride on Space Mountain is one of the few really
good memories I have of my father.

We spent three days at Disneyland, and during the trip I made it a point to take one, or both, of my older children on the ride.

Tristan was nine. I told him about my father and how much this ride meant to me. I told him how fun it was. I bought him a churro. I bought him popcorn. I got fast passes so we wouldn't have to wait in line. I begged him. I may have offered him a surprising amount of money to ride with me.

Sometime after he ate the churro and popcorn but before he accepted the money, Tristan refused.

"Too scary," he said.

I tried the same strategy with Norah, who was seven, and one year younger than I had been when my father took me. She pulled the same move, waiting until she'd eaten the snacks to turn me down.

I FELT A LITTLE USED, BUT I SUPPOSE FEELING USED IS A BIG PART OF FATHERHOOD. ONE WOULD ASSUME I'D BE USED TO IT NOW.

I should be proud of my children for their ability to maximize the preoffer before actually diving into a commitment they ultimately weren't interested in. But I wasn't proud of them. I was actually pretty pissed off about it.

I felt a little used, but I suppose feeling used is

a big part of fatherhood. One would assume I'd be used to it now.

Anyway, Mel had to watch our toddler, so she couldn't go. So . . . I rode it alone. Twice. Out of frustration. And a little spite. And because I had two fast passes.

I MET UP WITH MEL AND THE KIDS ONLY TO DISCOVER THAT NORAH WAS GETTING A MAKEOVER AT DISNEYLAND, SOMETHING I ASSUMED MUST HAVE COST BETWEEN TOO MUCH AND A BAZILLION DOLLARS.

The ride had changed a lot from what I remembered. It was all about Star Wars, that year. But there was a moment when I went through a lighted tube that I could still remember my father sitting ahead of me, his black hair slicked to the side, wearing a polo shirt, arms up, screaming. He was so alive that day. I was thrilled to be with him. I thought about how warm it felt to do something exciting with my father. I thought about how I wished my children would have ridden with me, so we could have relived this wonderful memory from my own childhood.

I walked across the park alone, feeling pretty let down.

This was supposed to be a highlight of the trip.

I met up with Mel and the kids only to discover

that Norah was getting a makeover at Disneyland, something I assumed must have cost between too much and a bazillion dollars. I immediately suspected that I'd been bamboozled.

Was going to Space Mountain alone a bait-and-switch sort of thing? Was it part of a larger plan laid out to distract me while my wife pampered our daughter?

Mel knows me well enough to understand that there was no way in hell I would've agreed to let Norah get a makeover at Disneyland. I'd have said it was too expensive. That we were spoiling her. That we'd already brought them to Disneyland, and taking her to get a makeover was going to set her up with astronomical over-the-top bratty expectations.

There were also my issues with Disney princesses in general. Three years earlier I published an essay in the *Huffington Post* titled, "My Daughter Is Not a Princess." This was when Norah was four and just starting to become infatuated with princesses. It was about how "I want her to grow up to be a well-rounded woman who values people for their qualities, not their possessions. I want her to love someone not because they own a castle or a nice horse, but because they are a good person with values and virtues. Someone who will not treat her like a princess, but treat her like a partner."

And, yes, I am aware of the irony that despite my feelings about Disney princesses, there we were at Disneyland, where all the princesses live. However, the main reason I wanted to visit the park was so I could ride on Space Mountain with my kids and relive the one good memory I had of my father. But now that had been spoiled, and I was struck with this fear that giving Norah a full-on princess makeover would turn her into some vapid turd of an adult, someone similar to Veruca Salt.

I know. I know. This all sounds over the top, but it really isn't all that far off from what I was thinking the moment Mel sent me a text reading, "We are at the Bibbidi Bobbidi Boutique getting Norah a makeover ;) Hope you don't mind. It's next to Sleeping Beauty's Castle."

I WAS STRUCK WITH THIS FEAR THAT GIVING NORAH A FULL-ON PRINCESS MAKEOVER WOULD TURN HER INTO SOME VAPID TURD OF AN ADULT, SOMEONE SIMILAR TO VERUCA SALT.

I did mind, actually. Her text might as well have read, "I distracted you so I could do something I knew you wouldn't agree with. Got ya, loser!"

I later discovered that Mel actually stumbled upon Bibbidi Bobbidi Boutique. There was no planning involved. It was an impulse thing, and her parents helped pay for the makeover. But in the moment, I didn't know any of that, so it all felt like a carefully played, cloak-and-dagger sort of thing.

At the Bibbidi Bobbidi Boutique, little girls get to pick what princess they'd like to be for the day (Norah picked Aurora), and then they get made-up head to toe to look like that princess. Fancy hairdo, glitter, tiara . . . the works. It also includes a photo shoot, a Disney princess meet and greet and the parents being called king and queen (that really is more of a side benefit).

I sat next to Mel on a bench in the Bibbidi Bobbidi Boutique gazing at my seven-year-old little girl. She was in a barber's chair, one woman doing her nails and another working on her hair, both dressed like secondary characters in a princess movie with plain blue dresses and shoes that were designed to look like they were made of wood. The whole time I was trying very hard not to be pissed at Mel, but failing, while she sat next to me with a smug ear-to-ear smile

I whispered a few things to her: "I wish you'd have consulted me first," and "I'm going to be honest right now, I'm not very comfortable with this," and "How much did this cost?"

She never answered any of my questions.

The whole time Mel simply patted my knee as though she knew something I didn't and kept looking forward, trying very hard not to miss a moment of Norah's makeover.

Norah was in a pink gown, a smile across her face, her small pink-and-white sneakers bouncing up and down, and I could see that whatever she was feeling was from her smile down to her toes. And once they placed a tiara on her head, they turned her around, her back to Mel and me, to face blue curtains with little plastic birds attached. One of the workers asked Norah if she was ready, and she couldn't seem to formulate the word *yes*, so she just nodded excitedly. The birds chirped and the curtains parted as though they'd been carried by the birds, revealing a gold-framed mirror.

Norah's life basically peaked in that moment. I've never seen her glow so brightly.

And then something happened. The second she saw herself I melted, from my head to my toes. I felt warmth in my heart. I felt a sense of wonder that, as a man, I have a difficult time defining or describing, but if I were going to try to give it a name, it would be a mix of pride and love. My eyes grew moist, not tears exactly, but something close.

Even as I'm writing this, the feeling is coming back.

As Norah turned around in her sparkly golden throne of a hairdresser's chair, we looked at each other, and suddenly I thought about Space Mountain. I thought about that one memory I had with my father and realized this trip wasn't about me.

It was about my kids.

Both Norah and I would remember that moment

for the rest of our lives. I had no doubt. Mel reached out and took my hand. We looked at each other, and she had a side smirk that seemed to say, "See?"

I leaned in and said, "This is my new favorite memory."

Mel smiled at me and said, "You're cute."

Then Norah crawled down from her chair, and I said, "Hello, Princess Aurora. Have you seen Norah? I've been looking for her."

Norah rolled her eyes and said, "Dad!"

I smiled at her, then crouched down, gave her a hug and said, "We need to get your picture taken."

She smiled and nodded. Then we walked outside hand in hand for her princess photo shoot.

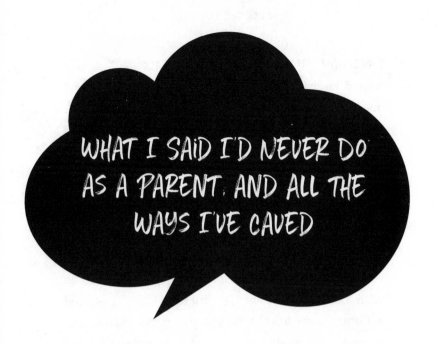

WHAT I SAID I'D NEVER DO AS A PARENT, AND ALL THE WAYS I'VE CAVED

Going into this whole fatherhood thing I had a pretty extensive list of dos and don'ts. I will be the first to admit that my list of don'ts was a lot longer than my dos. I had full intentions of making sure that my children presented themselves in a particular way and that all those little irritations that I witnessed in other child-parent dynamics were not going to be the case in my household. On the whole, I was a much better parent before I had kids.

How wrong I was.

Here are a few examples from my don't list.

I WILL NOT ALLOW MY CHILDREN TO TALK BACK. Every time I heard a child talk back to their parents, I made a promise, a commitment, an oath to myself that I'd never put up with that crap. But along came my children, with their opinions and their feelings, and their overall talk-back-ness that seems to crawl right up their throats, skipping their brains, and out their mouths. I've laid down punishments. I've said, "You don't talk to me like that," with such force and sincerity that all children in our neighborhood fell into line . . . except mine. But that's the issue with being a parent. My children know me well enough, they have felt out every boundary and crevice, and they know exactly how far to push things. They've seen every scrap of my inconsistencies, and they know when to pull back and when to push forward. But most importantly, now that I'm in this whole parenting thing, I've started to realize that sometimes when my children talk back, they're often on point, and I probably should listen. Sure, the tone and attitude is unfortunate, but sometimes my children are right.

I WILL NOT LET THEM DRESS LIKE MISMATCHED HOBOS. I used to look at kids in mismatched clothing and think my kids will not dress like that. But then, my kids started dressing themselves. One day, Norah came out of her room in a mixed-up outfit that included jeans, shorts, a skirt, clashing colors, flip-flops and a tiara. She was so proud of her outfit, and I was faced with the choice to support her exploration or squash her independence and make her change. I told her she looked fabulous and took her to the store.

THEY WILL NOT PLAY POKÉMON· For the sake of full transparency, I should probably admit that I never thought Pokémon would be around long enough for my children to enjoy it. I assumed that this ridiculous mythological animal-fighting show and all the various merchandise (cards, stuffed animals, apps, etc.) would have lost its appeal with my generation. But it hadn't.

I assumed that if a children's show irritated me, I'd ban it. I'd not allow it. I'd take that sucker out and push my children into something that I could tolerate. Once again, I felt like I had control over what my children did and didn't like, which is something all people think going into parenting, only to realize that parents can't even control when they sleep anymore. Children are going to be into whatever they want. Even if it irritates the crap out of you, as long as it's harmless, you just stop fighting and let it happen. Because the reality is, although I hate Pokémon with a passion, and I often fear that it's going to convince my children to move to South America and train animals to fight for sport, it keeps their attention long enough for me to take a shower, so I'm cool with it.

WE WILL NOT EAT AT McDONALD'S. There are so many reasons to hate McDonald's. The food is horrible. Ronald McDonald can't be trusted. The toys and fries are ruining my car. The play area is eerily sticky and smells like pee. I always said I'd never let my kids eat there but then Grandma stepped in. Mel's mother started taking Tristan there. He quickly became addicted to Happy Meals. Before he could speak, he could point at the golden arches and grunt. Then he'd cry when we didn't stop. Now, every time we eat out, both my older kids want to go to McDonald's. They love the place. I think there is nicotine in the fries or something. What I learned from all this is that when your kids love something, even though you think it's gross, sadly you end up there.

WE WILL NOT HAVE A MESSY BACK SEAT. Before having kids, I used to look at the back seat of parents' cars and wonder if they were hoarders. Now I understand that kids just don't care about your car. Our family van is like a moving dumpster. Sometimes it's like the back seat is another country with very liberal dumping laws.

WE WILL NOT PARTICIPATE IN SPORTS. I hated sports as a kid. I was a short, stocky young man with bad hand-eye coordination. Playing sports usually meant warming a bench or getting my trash kicked for missing a shot. But then my son came along, and as much as I hate sports, he loves them. As much as I despise giving up every Saturday to drive this sweaty, muddy little boy from soccer practice to games to another practice to another game, I cannot help but admit it has given him a drive and audacity that I never had at his age. So I do it because I know it's good for him. Sometimes parenting looks like giving up your weekends for something you hate because you can't help but grudgingly see how beneficial it is for your child.

Trust me, there's more. There always is. And there will be more, because that's what children do. They take every assumption you ever had and turn it on its head, and then suddenly you are left wondering who you are and what you stand for.

LET'S TALK ABOUT
POOP FOR A MOMENT

Norah showed me some dog poop in the front yard.
In the time it took me to walk to the backyard
for a shovel, Aspen grabbed the poop with her
little toddler hands and smeared it on her sister's
forearm. I didn't teach her to do that. I want to
get this across to you right now because I'm not
taking credit for my child's poop handling.

Norah ran into the house crying, Aspen chasing
her, me following the two with a shovel like
some sort of a gravedigger, not sure exactly what
happened during the five seconds I was in the
backyard but confident it had something to do with
the dog poop.

It all came to light quickly, however, when Aspen turned to me with blackish brown poop crammed between her little fingers, a hearty satisfied smile on her dimpled face. She was two, almost three, with shoulder-length blond hair that curled slightly at the tips. Her pink dress had a fluffy yellow cupcake on it. She wasn't wearing shoes.

I PRAY I'M NEVER IN A SITUATION WHERE MY LIFE DEPENDS ON ASPEN FINDING HER SHOES, BECAUSE I'D BE DEAD.

She never wears shoes.

I pray I'm never in a situation where my life depends on Aspen finding her shoes, because I'd be dead.

I dropped the shovel and put my hands out, hoping to push her back by the forehead, or chest, really anything to keep her hands away from me. We did an awkward dance. She lunged at me with her poop hands, and I swung my hips to one side then the other, trying to avoid her, Aspen giggling the whole time like we were playing a game.

But this was no game.

This was dog poop.

There are levels of poop, a hierarchy if you will: bird poop being at the bottom, baby poop around the middle and dog poop at the top of all-time nasty. Just looking at Aspen's hands made me want to gag.

I was terrified she'd touch me.

I was terrified that she might touch herself.

I was terrified that she'd eat it.

When it comes to young kids and poop, nothing is off the table.

I'VE COME INTO MY CHILDREN'S BEDROOM TO FIND POOP SMEARED ON THE WALLS AND FURNITURE AS IF THEY WERE SOME SORT OF POOP PICASSO. "HELLO, DADDY. I CALL THIS PAINTING 'LIFE IS SHIT'. WHAT DO YOU THINK?"

I never in a million years assumed parenting would involve incredible amounts of poop handling. I mean, maybe, in the back of my mind, I assumed there'd be a little poop. Perhaps cute, oh-the-baby-had-a-little-poopie kind of poop.

But I was wrong about that.

I've been wrong about a lot of things.

I've come into my children's bedroom to find poop smeared on the walls and furniture as if they were some sort of poop Picasso.

"Hello, Daddy. I call this painting 'Life is Shit.' What do you think?"

I've had them poop on the bathroom floor inches from the toilet, and then show it to me with a satisfied expression that seemed to say, "Look how close I got! Aren't you proud?"

I've had my children reach in the back of their loaded diaper, pull out a handful of poop and smear it across their face like war paint.

I shit you not.

When Tristan was two, he came down with some horrible virus that turned his bowels liquid. I remember him crying in the night. I came into his room and found him reaching from some bog like he was the son of the Swamp Thing, ankle deep in mushy goo.

I didn't want to touch him.

And I know. I know. I'm supposed to have compassion for what my child was going through. And sure, he was really sick. And I was worried about him. But at the same time, he was covered in poop. I don't care how much you love your kid, poop is still nasty. That never changes.

Part of me wanted to pretend like I never saw him and wait for my wife to handle it, but that would have been the ultimate dick move. After much turmoil, I eventually picked him up and carried him into the restroom.

We both needed a bath that night.

A few weeks before the dog poop incident, all three kids were playing in our backyard kid pool while Mel and I did yard work. Somewhere between the wheelbarrow and the weeds, when my back was turned, Aspen stripped from her Peppa Pig swimming suit and pooped in the backyard.

Tristan and Norah laughed.

I didn't.

I took Aspen inside to clean her up, and she pooped again, this time in the tub. Not as big as the first, but ultimately we have a no-poop policy in both the backyard and the tub, so even a little is too much.

I cleaned up both messes, gagging the whole time.

She didn't feel bad about this at all. Not one little bit. At one point she laughed at me. But why would she feel bad?

Ultimately it was my problem.

Poop always seems to be my problem, and when Aspen reached out for me with her dog poop hands, I knew this situation was no different.

Her eyes were on fire. She was so proud of herself for handling that dog poop.

As I danced around this little turd handler, she fell and cut her knee.

She cried long and hard, poop hands out for me to hold her. And suddenly I was faced with a decision. Leave her on the ground and forget that I have a daughter. Or pick her up and comfort her, all while getting dog poop on me.

I love Aspen, but in this moment I wanted to forget I ever had her. I wanted to leave her on the ground and just start over with another child.

Sometimes my kids are sick and dripping snot,

and they come at me like Jabba the Hutt asking Princess Leia for a kiss, and I pause for a moment, wondering if this whole parenting gig is really for me. Ultimately I kiss them, though. I always do. And sometimes they handle dog poop and cut their knee, and it's my job to make them right again.

So I did it.

Grudgingly.

I cleaned her hands and her cut, with her screaming the whole time and me crying on the inside. I sat her on my lap, all the while trying desperately not to get poop on me but failing.

No one gave me a pat on the back.

No one gave me an award.

Chances are, she won't even remember this moment.

But I know I did the right thing.

Once Aspen was settled, with clean hands and a Band-Aid on her knee, she gave me a hug.

Then she wandered into the yard, probably searching for more poop.

I BOUGHT A MINIVAN (EPIC EYE ROLL)

Although I understood the reasoning for buying a minivan, I really didn't like the idea because buying a van made me feel like a 30-something nerdy father. Which, I admit, I am—but I didn't want to look like one. I still wanted to feel "with it." I wanted young people to look at me and think that I'm cool or sexy or cool and sexy. I wanted to feel young, but I didn't want all the hassle that comes with being young. I was comfortable in my marriage and my job, but at the same time, I still wanted to feel fancy-free. And I think that's the problem with buying a minivan.

It felt like I was giving up something that I couldn't define. My youth? My coolness? I didn't know, but what I do know is that during the drive to the car lot to shop for a van, I felt nervous. Next to me was my wife of over a decade, and in the back seat were my three children. I had a big-kid after-college job and a mortgage, and when I added up all those things, I did look a lot like an adult on paper.

As we drove, I told myself that my anxiety was because we were planning to make a major purchase.

But that wasn't the problem.

I was nervous when we bought our house. And I was nervous to become a father and get married and all that other big-kid stuff. But it was a different kind of nervous when we bought the van, and I think it had to do with how I'd always said I'd never be one of "those minivan parents."

We bought a red Mazda5 in a town 30 miles away, and as I drove it home, I felt horrible. We chose the Mazda5 because it had good *Consumer Reports* ratings, and it was within our budget, but we really chose it because it was a smaller sporty-looking van that if caught at the right angle didn't exactly look like a van. It wasn't a bubble-looking thing with a big butt in the back that made everyone behind me know for a fact that there was a baby on board regardless of whether or not we hung a sign in the window.

Regardless of how sleek it was, as I drove the van home I wished we'd just gotten a bigger car or perhaps an SUV of some kind. Something with four-wheel drive. Something a little more badass. But we had three kids, and cramming them all in our small Protegé felt like cramming clowns in a Smart Car. It just wasn't working, and although I didn't feel as nerdy driving our car around town, it was impractical (like most things that are cool).

And I guess that's the hardest part about getting older. I now value what's practical over what's cool. It seems like everything I do as a parent is practical. All of my decisions. In 2016, a few months before Christmas, the Misfits, one of my favorite punk bands, reunited in Chicago. I genuinely considered going. Sure, the whole band is close to 60 now, which is ten years after doctors recommend a colonoscopy. I mean, really, how badass could they still be?

> AND I GUESS THAT'S THE HARDEST
> PART ABOUT GETTING OLDER. I NOW
> VALUE WHAT'S PRACTICAL OVER WHAT'S
> COOL. IT SEEMS LIKE EVERYTHING
> I DO AS A PARENT IS PRACTICAL.
> ALL OF MY DECISIONS.

I'm confident I'd have left the concert with a permanently injured back. But it would have been so fun to cast off my obligations and fly to a big city to see a band I really loved. But then I started thinking about how we were saving money for Christmas, and ultimately I imagined a conversation with my children where my wife had to lean forward and say, "We had plans to give you a wonderful Christmas, but Dad spent that money seeing an old punk band in Chicago. Now he needs back surgery."

What a dick move that would've been.

But it was one of many rational and ultimately very uncool choices I'd been making over the years.

Buying the minivan was all part of a long list of gradual sacrifices I'd made in the name of being practical.

For example, when I finished my master's in 2012, at age 29, I found a job in Oregon. We were living in Minnesota, and it was going to be a huge move, halfway across the United States. We had a yard sale to get rid of some things.

Having a full-time job made me feel a little more grown-up, and I had a desire to let go of the past. I added punk band memorabilia to the sale: T-shirts, belt buckles, pins and patches. And as I dug out these mementos, I also dug out my old CD collection.

I stopped attending concerts shortly after Tristan was born, but I still had my music. Hundreds of CDs that I stored in a large cardboard box in our garage. I collected them before I got married, many before the Internet. They represented hours in used music stores, searching through CD racks to find obscure punk bands that I'd heard rumor of but never listened to. They represented punk shows at sketchy venues: bowling alleys, abandoned ware-houses and bars, where I purchased albums from skinny-looking roadies.

They were the tangible evidence of a cool and rebellious life before I became a buttoned-up husband and father.

I cracked open the box, rooted through it for a bit and suddenly I felt the need to add it to the sale. It seemed like a symbol. I was growing up. It felt right.

I put it in the yard with a sign on it that read "CDs $1 Each." I thought I might sell a few albums. Probably just the trendy stuff. It'll help out the family and lighten the load.

I felt good about that.

I really did.

Pat-myself-on-the-back kind of good.

I left the yard sale for a moment to get something from the car. We lived in a townhome, and I had to walk a good distance to get to the parking lot. I was gone for about ten minutes, and when I came back Mel said, "I sold your box of CDs."

She didn't say it with spite or anger. She didn't say it like she'd won a huge victory. She said it innocently. She said it with a hint of compassion because she knew how much they meant to me.

"I hope that's okay," she said.

I felt a deep hurt in my heart. My hands started to shake a little. I didn't know what to say, so I said the obvious. "How much did you sell them for?"

"Ten dollars," she said.

My knees got weak. I wanted to yell, *You sold all my punk albums for ten dollars? Do you know how long it took me to find those? Do you know what they meant to me? Do you even care about my youth?*

But I didn't because this whole scene was familiar.

When I was thirteen years old, in 1995, my older brother, Ryan, was a round-faced stocky kid who wore tank tops and sported a flattop mullet. I had a bowl cut and a buck-toothed smile. We went to a yard sale a few miles from our home in rural Utah and found a box of records. A woman, probably in her mid-30s, was running the sale. She had bangs with a big '80s-style perm. The records were mostly Whitesnake, but there were a couple of Clash and Ramones albums.

We bought the whole box for a couple of bucks. Ryan balanced it on the handlebars of his bike so we could get it home. And as we rode off, I could hear a man yelling in the background, "You sold all my Whitesnake records!"

He yelled it a couple of times. His voice had a southern twang that only amplified his pain.

Ryan and I rode faster. I assumed it was the woman's husband, and I recall thinking that he sounded pathetic. He sounded like some loser living in the past. I even said to Ryan, "That guy needs to grow up."

Flash forward fifteen years and suddenly I was

that guy, angry because his wife sold his youth. Instead of yelling at Mel, I went into our Minnesota townhouse, sat on my bed and placed my face in my hands. I wanted to cry, but I couldn't muster the strength. I had to use all my energy to keep from getting angry and wind up looking like that long-haired Whitesnake fan from my youth.

I sulked in our room for a while until I felt confident enough to go back outside and help with the yard sale.

REGARDLESS OF THE ERA, PARENTHOOD SEEMS TO HAVE A PRETTY STANDARD TRAJECTORY, WHERE EVERY-THING PARENTS DO TO TRY TO REMAIN YOUNG AND COOL GETS TORN OUT FROM UNDER THEM UNTIL THEY ARE SITTING IN A RECLINER, WEARING A POLO SHIRT AND CARGO SHORTS AND YELLING, 'SHUT THE DOOR! YOU'RE LETTING THE HEAT OUT!'

I'm, like, 90 percent sure that Whitesnake fan had a minivan in his yard, and when I think about that, I realize that he was going through the same changes I was, only he got the van first and sold his albums second. Regardless of the era, parenthood seems to have a pretty standard trajectory, where everything parents do to try to remain young and cool gets torn out from under them until they are sitting in a recliner, wearing a polo shirt and cargo shorts and yelling, "Shut the door! You're letting the heat out!"

I assumed that if I held on to what I thought was cool, I'd never become what I'd always dreaded: a dorky father. But it doesn't work that way because parents are uncool by definition, and when parents try to stay cool, they become that guy in the '90s still sporting a mullet and listening to Whitesnake, or, in my case, that guy in 2012 still holding on to his Blink-182 albums, band patches and baggy JNCO jeans. I'd become an anachronism, living in my own bubble, stuck in the era where I was coolest, while everyone around me thought, "You need to grow up."

Two weeks into having a minivan, here's what I found out: Although I looked like an old fart in the thing, I'd never felt more comfortable traveling with my children. We had room for *all* their crap. We could seat them far enough away from each other that they couldn't kick or punch or touch. When it rained, I could climb in the sucker to help buckle the kids and not get wet. I could fit all my groceries in the back, along with a stroller and an open case of Diet Mountain Dew. The sliding doors made it easy to get the kids in and out, and no one had to crawl over a sibling when exiting.

It was a wonderful decision to get one, and although it felt like I made the transition from fashionable clothing to SAS shoes, slacks and suspenders, I don't know how I'd ever lived without it.

And you know what? Realizing that was a turning point.

I was letting go of youth.

I stopped looking at who I was, and began to look at who I was becoming.

I was on a new road with a new perception in a new van, so I rolled down all the windows and let the air drift across my receding hairline.

It sounded better than any concert.

It felt better than my first kiss.

I savored the moment, breathed it, until my children yelled at me for making the van cold, so I rolled the windows up again.

IT GOES BY PRETTY FAST.
STOP AND LOOK AROUND.

A few weeks after Tristan turned ten, I was sitting on his bed working on my laptop. Tristan's head was in my lap, and I kept my laptop close to my knees to make room for him. He was breathing into my thigh, dead asleep. Meanwhile, my leg was falling asleep, too, and as I watched him, I wondered how many more of these moments we had left.

He used to ask me to sit next to him while he fell asleep every night. And most nights I told him that I didn't have time. When I was in college, I told him I had to work on a term paper or read a few chapters from some college text or pack my lunch for the next day or fold some laundry.

I can still see him standing in the hallway, two feet tall, in his black-and-red dump truck pajamas, barefoot, one small hand cupped in the other, eyes looking down.

"You need to be a big kid and go to sleep on your own," I said.

I told him that a lot. I thought I was teaching him to be independent.

But now, I don't know if that's really true.

I WAS LEFT WITH THE CLEAR UNDERSTANDING THAT GETTING HIT BY A CAR WAS LESS THREATENING THAN HIS FRIENDS SEEING HIM HUG ME.

With each year, he drifts further away from me. He doesn't like me to hug him in front of his friends anymore. I once dropped him off at school, and as I leaned down to give him a hug goodbye, he ran away from me, across the school parking lot without looking both ways, and was nearly clipped by a car. Once I was done feeling terrified, I was left with the clear understanding that getting hit by a car was less threatening than his friends seeing him hug me.

He gets embarrassed when I call him by one of his nicknames: Gooey or Goober Kid. He doesn't climb into my lap when I sit on the sofa, or snuggle next to me when we watch a movie. Most of the time he sits on the floor a few feet away, his back to me.

He doesn't pull at my pant leg to get attention or sit on my foot so I can drag him around. He doesn't ask to talk to me on the phone anymore when I call the house, and then tell me a plot summary of the latest installment of *Go, Diego, Go!* I used to lock the bedroom door so I could work on my writing, and he'd stick his little pink fingers under the door and ask if I could see them. He'd invite me to play in the yard through the keyhole. I don't even have to lock the door now.

In fact, he locks his door now. I'm the one knocking and asking if he wants to play in the yard.

I'm the one sticking my fingers under the door.

He doesn't find that funny at all. Not one little bit.

He used to greet me with a big hug at the end of the driveway when I got home from work.

Now he just asks if he can play with the iPad.

Most of his life he begged and pleaded and tugged for my attention, but suddenly he seemed to be drifting away. Taking those steps toward independence that I wanted him to take so badly, and now that he has, I want him back.

I want him to snuggle with me on the sofa again. I want to see him light up and run to the door as I step into the house.

I think part of the problem is that I wanted his attention on my terms. I wanted him to tug on my pant leg when I didn't have anything important to do, when I had time to be distracted. I wanted him to get on the phone when I wasn't in a hurry to deliver some message to my wife, and then hang up and get on with this or that. I wanted him to sit on my lap when there wasn't a textbook or a laptop on it. I wanted him to be my son when it was convenient.

> MOST OF HIS LIFE HE BEGGED AND PLEADED AND TUGGED FOR MY ATTENTION, BUT SUDDENLY HE SEEMED TO BE DRIFTING AWAY. TAKING THOSE STEPS TOWARD INDEPENDENCE THAT I WANTED HIM TO TAKE SO BADLY, AND NOW THAT HE HAS, I WANT HIM BACK.

But when was I free to be distracted?

We had Tristan when I was 24 years old. I was a late bloomer, and I had been in college for only two years. The first five years of his life I struggled to make ends meet while attending classes.

If I didn't have something I needed to do for school or work, there was always something I wanted to do, and rarely as a young father did the things I wanted to do involve Tristan. They involved long bike rides and writing projects, or watching movies or reading books that Tristan couldn't understand.

I went to the gym, or I went backpacking with friends. Sometimes I went to concerts.

Tristan, well, he kind of got what was left, which wasn't nearly enough.

Even though I told myself that everything I was doing was to make his life better, what it came down to was that I wasn't making time for him. Plain and simple.

I often boast about going through college with kids. I use it as a way to get the college students I work with to stop complaining. But looking back, I feel like I was a full-time student, a full-time employee and a half-assed father.

It's only now that I'm finished with graduate school and working a full-time job that I have become more reflective and started to realize all the moments I've lost with my young son. So much of everything I did in my twenties was an attempt to find a comfortable and stable career so I could take care of my family. But looking back, I made a lot of sacrifices along the way.

I was pushing my son away.

And now, I want those moments back.

Now I'm the one tugging at his sleeve, asking if he wants to watch a movie or play outside. Now I'm the one sitting on the floor, trying to snuggle next to him, and hearing him say, "Go away, Dad. I'm busy."

I'm the one asking to talk to him on the phone when I call home, only to sit on the line asking questions and getting a yes and a no and then handed an excuse to hang up. I'm the one asking if he wants to play catch in the yard.

I'm the one running to meet him at the door.

It feels like Tristan and I are on different trajectories now, me trying to make up for the time I missed with him while I was in college, and him trying to get away from his embarrassing father.

And the harder I try, the more he pushes back. The more he tells me to leave him alone.

But sometimes he gets scared, like the night when I was sitting next to him in his bed, and he snuggled up next to me and fell asleep.

Sometimes he's still that little boy who needs me.

It's then that I feel like I'm getting some of those moments back. I feel like Tristan is that little four-year-old boy lying next to me on his bed, gazing up at the stars broadcast from his stuffed light-up turtle, the two of us making up constellations.

"That one looks like Diego," he'd say.

"Sure," I'd say, "Sure. I've got to go work on a paper."

I jump on those moments now.

I suppose what I'm trying to say is that I learned a lot in college. I learned how to write and read and think critically. I learned how to get things done. But most importantly, I learned that the moments I sacrificed in college and away from my son are gone forever, and I want to savor the moments we have left.

I looked down at Tristan sleeping soundly. I gently moved his head to the side and then slipped out of his bed. I gathered my things, and as I shut the door, he stirred. He looked up at me with glassy confused eyes and said, "Don't go. I'm scared."

It was late. I had to be up in the morning. I wanted to take a shower and get to bed. Instead, I set my things on the floor and sat next to him again. He snuggled next to me, his head resting on my ribs, his arms across my stomach.

Then he fell asleep.

Eventually, I did too.

ACKNOWLEDGMENTS

First and foremost, my wife, Melodie Edwards. Thank you for your honesty, for reading my drafts, letting me write so openly about our lives, insisting that I can, and for Tristan, Norah and Aspen.

A huge thank you to Geoff Herbach. You started out as my MFA thesis advisor and have become a friend and coconspirator. Every time I'm faced with something new as a writer, I message you. And you always respond. I can't tell you how much that means.

Thank you Marissa Giambelluca, my editor, for your time, effort and careful comments. I know I was pretty pissed after that first round of edits, but once that all settled, you helped me write the way I wanted to when I started writing. That's pretty amazing.

William Kiester, thank you for helping me develop this concept and taking a risk on a humorously anxious new author.

Thank you to Jill Smokler, Samantha Angoletta and all the good people over at Scary Mommy. You helped me build my audience. You helped me find my people.

To the followers of *No Idea What I'm Doing: A Daddy Blog*, you keep me writing. Thank you for finding me interesting. I honestly love sharing my experiences with you. And in doing so, I learn a lot about my family and myself.

Thank you to the very talented writing instructors at Utah Valley University for giving me my creative beginnings.

Thank you to the MFA faculty at Minnesota State University, Mankato, for your influence and support.

Mom, Melissa, Ryan and Kip (my fam): I know you don't really understand why I write, but thank you for trying to understand.

Thank you to the good people at Page Street.

Lastly, I'd like to thank God for, you know, everything.

ABOUT
THE AUTHOR

Clint Edwards is the author of the funny and insightful *No Idea What I'm Doing: A Daddy Blog*. He is a staff writer for the very popular (and awesome) Scary Mommy. His work has been discussed on *Good Morning America*, *The View*, *The Talk* and *Today*. Everyone from Whoopi Goldberg to Sharon Osbourne to Kathie Lee Gifford has agreed with his take on parenting and marriage. He's also a parenting contributor to the *New York Times*, the *Washington Post*, the *Huffington Post*, Disney's Babble and elsewhere.